Math
Expressions

Assessment Guide

Developed by
The Children's Math Worlds Research Project

PROJECT DIRECTOR AND AUTHOR
Dr. Karen C. Fuson

This material is based upon work supported by the
National Science Foundation
under Grant Numbers
ESI-9816320, REC-9806020, and RED-935373.

Any opinions, findings, and conclusions, or recommendations expressed in this material
are those of the author and do not necessarily reflect the views of the National Science Foundation.

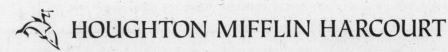

Teacher Reviewers

Kindergarten

Patricia Stroh Sugiyama
Wilmette, Illinois

Barbara Wahle
Evanston, Illinois

Grade 1

Sandra Budson
Newton, Massachusetts

Janet Pecci
Chicago, Illinois

Megan Rees
Chicago, Illinois

Grade 2

Molly Dunn
Danvers, Massachusetts

Agnes Lesnick
Hillside, Illinois

Rita Soto
Chicago, Illinois

Grade 3

Jane Curran
Honesdale, Pennsylvania

Sandra Tucker
Chicago, Illinois

Grade 4

Sara Stoneberg Llibre
Chicago, Illinois

Sheri Roedel
Chicago, Illinois

Grade 5

Todd Atler
Chicago, Illinois

Leah Barry
Norfolk, Massachusetts

Credits

Cover art: © Arco Images GmbH/Alamy.

Illustrative art: Schawk Inc.
Technical art: Schawk Inc.

Printed in the U.S.A.

ISBN: 978-0-547-06707-0

3 4 5 6 7 8 9 EB 17 16 15 14 13 12 11 10 09

TABLE OF CONTENTS

Class Record Sheet
Beginning of Year Inventory

Name of Student	Number and Operations	Algebra	Geometry	Measurement	Data Analysis and Probability

I1

Grade 5 Inventory Test Correlation

Inventory Test Item	NCTM Standard	Grade 4 Unit Learning Goals
1	Number and Operations	4.1.2
2	Number and Operations	4.3.4
3–4	Number and Operations	4.3.8
5	Number and Operations	4.3.12
6	Number and Operations	4.3.18
7	Number and Operations	4.3.1, 4.5.2
8	Number and Operations	4.3.2, 4.5.3
9	Number and Operations	4.3.3, 4.5.8
10–11	Number and Operations	4.5.10
12	Number and Operations	4.7.1, 4.7.2
13–14	Number and Operations	4.7.7
15	Number and Operations	4.9.11
16	Number and Operations	4.9.20
17	Number and Operations	4.5.1, 4.9.7, 4.9.9, 4.9.12
18	Number and Operations	4.9.17
19	Number and Operations	4.11.2
20	Number and Operations	4.11.3
21	Number and Operations	4.11.6
22	Number and Operations	4.6.3, 4.11.9, 4.11.10
23–24	Algebra	4.FP.16
25	Algebra	4.7.5
26	Algebra	4.8.2
27–28	Algebra	4.8.3
29	Geometry	4.2.1
30	Geometry	4.2.2
31–32	Geometry	4.4.3
33	Geometry	4.4.6
34	Geometry	4.9.5
35	Geometry	4.10.1
36	Geometry	4.10.2
37	Measurement	4.2.6
38	Measurement	4.4.5
39	Measurement	4.6.1
40	Measurement	4.6.3
41	Measurement	4.7.10
42	Measurement	4.12.5
43	Measurement	4.12.2

Grade 5 Inventory Test Correlation

Inventory Test Item	NCTM Standard	Grade 4 Unit Learning Goals
44	Measurement	4.12.1
45	Data Analysis and Probability	4.1.4, 4.1.5
46–47	Data Analysis and Probability	4.7.8
48	Data Analysis and Probability	4.9.6
49	Data Analysis and Probability	4.8.5
50	Data Analysis and Probability	4.9.15

Inventory Test Correlation

Number and Operations

Solve. Label your answer.

1. Randee has 5 shirts and 7 pairs of pants.
   How many different outfits can she make?

   _____ 35 outfits _____

2. Write an equation using a letter to represent
   the unknown. Then solve. Brianna walked for
   35 minutes on Saturday. She walked for a total
   of 68 minutes for the weekend. How many minutes
   did she walk on Sunday?

   _____ $35 + m = 68$; $m = 33$ minutes _____

3. Write each number in standard form.

   two million, five hundred forty-six thousand,
   three hundred seventy-five   _____ 2,546,375 _____

   six thousand forty-two   _____ 6,042 _____

Round to the nearest thousand.

4. 43,464 _____ 43,000 _____

Copy each exercise, lining up the places correctly.
Then add or subtract.

5. $3,542 + 4,009 =$ _____ 7,551 _____   6. $13,228 - 10,109 =$ _____ 3,119 _____

7. Use mental math to find each product.

   a. $2 \times 6 =$ _____12_____

   b. $2 \times 60 =$ _____120_____

   c. $20 \times 60 =$ _____1200_____

8. Multiply using any method. Show your work.

   a. $72 \times 3 =$ _____216_____   **b.** $607 \times 7 =$ _____4,249_____

9. Estimate each product.

   a. $62 \times 47 =$ _____3,000_____   **b.** $18 \times 400 =$ _____8,000_____

Solve each problem. List any extra numerical information.

10. Two classes are collecting winter gloves for charity.
There are 21 students in one class and 18 students
in the other class. Each student collected 5 pairs
of gloves. How many pairs of gloves did the two
classes collect altogether?

Show your work.

_____195 pairs of gloves_____

11. A family spent 3 hours at the movie theater.
They bought two adult tickets for $8 each and
two children's tickets for $5 each. They spent $12
on food. How much did they spend in all at
the movies?

_____$38; Extra information: 3 hours at the theater_____

12. Find each quotient.

a. $3\overline{)29}$ 9 R2

b. $4\overline{)247}$ 61 R3

c. $6\overline{)4,018}$ 669 R4

d. $2\overline{)16,771}$ 8,385 R1

Solve. Use rounding and estimation to decide whether the answer makes sense. Explain your work.

Show your work.

13. Gianna cut a 36-inch rope into 7 equal pieces. How long was each piece?

$36 \div 7 = 5\frac{1}{7}$ inches long; $5 \times 7 = 35$;

the answer makes sense.

14. A worker at the bookstore needs to take 2,764 books out of boxes. At the end of the weekend, there were 1,076 books still left in boxes. How many books did the worker take out of the boxes over the weekend?

$2,764 - 1,076 = 1,688$; $2,800 - 1,100 = 1,700$;

the answer makes sense.

15. Write 4 fractions equivalent to $\frac{3}{4}$.

Answers will vary. Possible answers are given.

$\frac{6}{8}$ $\frac{9}{12}$ $\frac{12}{16}$ $\frac{15}{20}$

16. Label the point for each fraction or mixed number with the corresponding letter.

A $1\frac{1}{6}$ *B* $3\frac{1}{3}$ *C* $\frac{1}{2}$ *D* $4\frac{5}{6}$

17. Add or subtract.

a. $\frac{2}{5} + \frac{3}{5} = \frac{5}{5}$

b. $3\frac{1}{2} - \frac{3}{4} = 2\frac{3}{4}$

c. $3\frac{4}{6} + 1\frac{3}{6} = 5\frac{1}{6}$

18. Multiply.

a. $4 \times \frac{1}{5} =$ _____ $\frac{4}{5}$

b. $12 \times \frac{3}{4} =$ _____ 9

c. $\frac{1}{5} \times 25 =$ _____ 5

19. **a.** Write the decimal number in words.

45.33

forty-five and thirty-three hundredths

b. Write the decimal number.

Seven and two hundredths

7.02

20. Insert >, <, or = to make a true statement.

a. 0.456 $\boxed{<}$ 0.478

b. 1.6 $\boxed{>}$ 1.46

c. 0.220 $\boxed{=}$ 0.22

21. Round the number to the nearest tenth and to the nearest whole number.
5.31

a. nearest tenth: _5.3_

b. nearest whole number: _5_

22. Add or subtract.

a. 5.067 + 0.4 = _5.467_

b. 8.11 − 4.08 = _4.03_

Algebra

23. Use the Commutative Property of Multiplication to find the value of n.

a. $9 \times 5 = 5 \times n$ $n =$ ___9___

b. $8 \times 2 = 2 \times n$ $n =$ ___8___

24. Name the property used in each equation.

a. $1 \bullet 17 = 17$ b. $(3 \times 4) \times 5 = 3 \times (4 \times 5)$

___Identity Property of___   ___Associative Property___
___Multiplication___   ___of Multiplication___

25. Solve.

a. $a \bullet 8 = 48$ b. $56 - m = 11$ c. $6 \bullet (11 - p) = 54$
   $a =$ ___6___ $m =$ ___45___ $p =$ ___2___

26. Write the rule, and use it to complete the function table.

Rule: multiply the input by 9, or divide the output by 9							
Input	4	8	10	12	1	9	5	7
Output	36	72	90	108| 9	81	45	63

Use the coordinate plane.

27. Plot a point in the coordinate plane
at each location.

   a. (5, 8)

   b. (6, 2)

28. Write an ordered pair to represent
the location of each point.

   a. Point *R* _____(3, 7)_____

   b. Point *P* _____(9, 4)_____

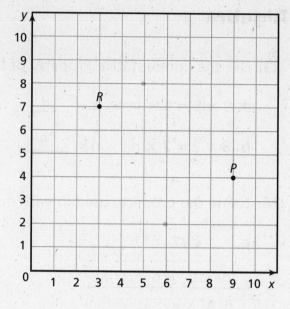

Beginning of the Year Test

Geometry

29. Draw a figure that is congruent to the one shown.

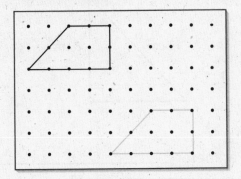

30. Describe the figure.

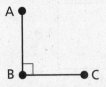

perpendicular line segments

AB and BC meeting at a right

angle at point B

Name each triangle by its angles. Explain your thinking.

31.

right triangle

1 right angle

32.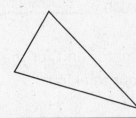

acute triangle

3 acute angles

---

33. Name the regular polygon and find the perimeter.

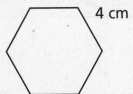 4 cm

hexagon

_24 cm_

---

34. Label each part of the circle.

radius

center

circumference

diameter

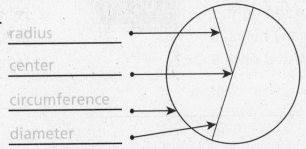

---

35. Name the solid.

sphere

36. Name the solid you can build from this net.

cylinder

Measurement

Find the perimeter and area of each figure.

37.

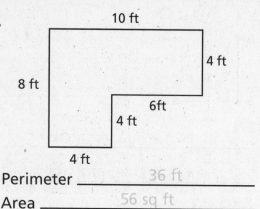

10 ft

4 ft

8 ft

6ft

4 ft

4 ft

Perimeter _____ 36 ft _____
Area _____ 56 sq ft _____

38.

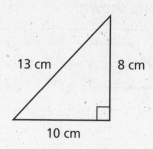

13 cm   8 cm

10 cm

Perimeter _____ 31 cm _____
Area _____ 40 sq cm _____

39. Write the correct metric unit to complete the equation.

10 meters = 10,000 _____ millimeters _____

40. Write the best metric unit for the amount of juice a pitcher can hold. Explain your thinking.

Liters; a pitcher holds a medium amount of liquid, so milliliters are too small to measure its capacity.

41. Look at the digital clock to the right. How many hours have passed since 9 P.M.?

3:00 A.M.

6 hours

42. On Monday, it was 65 degrees Fahrenheit at 8 A.M. and 89 degrees at 8 P.M. How many degrees did the temperature rise?

24 degrees

43. How many cubic feet are in 3 cubic yards?

81 cubic feet

44. Draw a line segment that is $1\frac{3}{4}$ inches long.

Data Analysis and Probability

The bar graph shows the number of tickets sold at the fair each day.

45. a. How many more tickets were sold on Sunday than on Saturday?

20 tickets

b. On which day did they sell $\frac{1}{2}$ as many tickets as on Sunday?

Friday

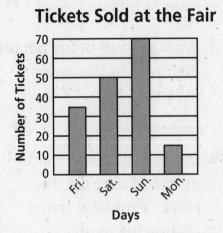

Tickets Sold at the Fair

46. On his four races, Matt had finishing times of 47 seconds, 52 seconds, 51 seconds, and 46 seconds. What was his mean time?

47 + 52 + 51 + 46 = 196; 196 ÷ 4 = 49 seconds

Show your work.

47. Use the data set below.

{12, 25, 14, 12, 10, 16, 12, 15, 14}

a. What is the mode? _____12_____

b. What is the median? _____14_____

Use the circle graph to answer the questions. Show your work.

48. There are 16 students in the class. How many students prefer each pizza topping?

Cheese ____8 students____

Peppers ____2 students____

Onions ____2 students____

Chicken ____4 students____

Pizza Topping Preferences for Our Class

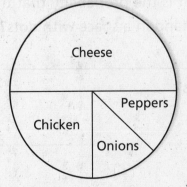

Use the line graph.

49. The line graph shows the mayor's approval rating during his first six months in office.

a. What percent of the population approved of the mayor in January?

_90%_

b. During which one-month period of time did the mayor's approval rating change the most?

June to July

c. Was the change in exercise b. above an increase or decrease?

increase

d. Using the data in the graph, can you predict if the mayor's approval rating will increase or decrease in August? Support your answer.

Accept any answer that has well-reasoned support. Sample:

No. The mayor's approval rating has gone up and down,

and you cannot tell what it might do in August.

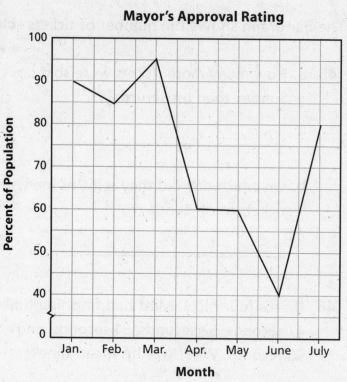

Mayor's Approval Rating

Percent of Population

Month

50. Suppose you spin this spinner once. What is the probability that the spinner will land in a space with dots?

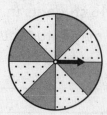

$\frac{4}{8}$ or $\frac{1}{2}$

1. For the function table, write the rule in words and as an equation. Then complete the table.

Rule in words: Number of players equals number of teams times 9.					
Equation: $p = 9t$					
Teams (t)	1	2	3	4	5
Players (p)	9	18	27	36	45

Solve.

2. Tina has saved 7 quarters. Each week her parents will give her 5 more quarters. How many quarters will Tina have after 4 weeks?

   27 quarters; $7 + (5 \times 4) = 27$

3. There were 21 adults at the school meeting. That number is 3 times as many as the number of students at the meeting. How many students attended the meeting?

   7 students; $\frac{1}{3} \times 21 = 7$

4. Katria saw 3 types of flowers in the botanical garden—tulips, roses, and daffodils. She saw 3 times as many tulips as roses and 4 times as many daffodils as roses. Altogether there are 72 flowers. How many of each kind of flower did she see?

   $r + 3r + 4r = 72$; 9 roses, 27 tulips, 36 daffodils

5. Which Multiplication Property can be used to find the missing number in the equation? Find the missing number. Explain.

   $(263 \times 487) \times 952 = n \times (487 \times 952)$

   Associative Property; 263; Possible explanation: Only the grouping symbols changed, the numbers stayed in the same places. 263 was the only number missing from the left side.

Name all the factor pairs for each number.

1. 17 _____1 and 17_____   2. 20 __1 and 20; 2 and 10; 4 and 5__

3. 18 __1 and 18; 2 and 9; 3 and 6__   4. 40 __1 and 40; 2 and 20; 4 and 10, 5 and 8__

Complete each equation.

5. If 3(4 + 2) = 18, then (3 • 4) + (3 • __2__) = 18

6. If $a \times b$ is 124, then $b \times a$ must be __124__.

7. A bus holds 36 people. There are 9 identical rows of seats. How many people can sit in each row? ___4 people___.

8. John planted 64 flowers in a square in his garden. There are 8 flowers across one side of the square. How many flowers are along an adjacent side of the square? ___8 flowers___.

9. A sandwich shop has 3 kinds of bread, 5 kinds of fillings, and 2 kinds of potato chips. How many different lunch combinations are there? ___30 combinations___.

For each function table, write the rule in words and as an equation. Then complete the table.

10.

Rule in words: Output equals input times 5.					
Equation: $O = I \times 5$					
Input	1	2	3	4	5	6
Output	5	10	15	20	25	30

1.

Rule in words: Number of legs equals number of spiders times 8.				
Equation: $l = 8s$				
Spiders (s)	1	2	3	4	5
Legs (l)	8	16	24	32	40

Solve each equation.

12. $6r = 42$
$r = \underline{\ 7\ }$

13. $40 = 10w$
$w = \underline{\ 4\ }$

14. $50 \times 0 = s$
$s = \underline{\ 0\ }$

15. $f = 45 - (3 \bullet 5)$
$f = \underline{\ 30\ }$

Use the Properties of Multiplication to solve for n.

16. $(335 \times 426) \times 205 = n \times (426 \times 205)$
$n = \underline{\ 335\ }$

17. $1{,}598 \times 675 = n \times 1{,}598$
$n = \underline{\ 675\ }$

Solve.

18. Clara, Eddy, and Bill collect cans to recycle. Eddy has 12 cans. Clara has 4 times as many cans as Eddy. Bill has 2 times as many cans as Clara. How many cans does Bill have?

96 cans

Show your work.

19. Gino bought 4 pencils for 6 cents each, and 2 erasers for 4 cents each. How much money did Gino spend?

32 cents

20. Extended Response Sally wants to buy a cover for her pool. Her pool is an odd shape made up of a rectangle and a triangle. The rectangular part of her pool is 8 meters by 6 meters. The triangular part has a height of 4 meters and a base of 5 meters. What is the area of the pool cover Sally will buy? Explain how you solved the problem.

Possible Explanation: The area of the rectangular

part of the pool is $6 \bullet 8 = 48$ sq m. The area of the

triangular part of the pool is $(5 \bullet 4) \div 2 = 10$ sq m.

The area of the pool cover is $48 + 10 = 58$ sq m.

Fill in the circle for the correct answer.

Which set of numbers includes all the factors for the given number?

1. 16

Ⓐ 1, 3, 5, 16
Ⓑ 1, 2, 4, 8, 16
Ⓒ 2, 4, 8, 16
Ⓓ 2, 4, 8

2. 31

Ⓕ 1, 2, 15, 31
Ⓖ 0, 1, 31
Ⓗ 31
Ⓚ 1, 31

3. 24

Ⓐ 1, 2, 3, 4, 6, 8, 12, 24
Ⓑ 1, 2, 4, 6, 12
Ⓒ 2, 3, 4, 6, 8, 12
Ⓓ 1, 24

4. 32

Ⓕ 1, 32
Ⓖ 1, 2, 4, 8, 18, 32
Ⓗ 1, 2, 4, 8, 16, 32
Ⓚ 2, 4, 8, 16

Which number makes the equation true?

5. If $(7 \cdot 8) + (7 \cdot 6) = 98$, then $7(\underline{\hspace{1cm}} + 6) = 98$

Ⓐ 6   Ⓑ 7   Ⓒ 8   Ⓓ 9

6. If $a \times b = 112$, then $b \times a$ must be _____.

Ⓕ 121   Ⓖ 112   Ⓗ 100   Ⓚ 211

Solve.

7. Jan has an array of stamps. There are 20 stamps in all. There are 5 stamps in each row. How many rows are there?

Ⓐ 3   Ⓑ 4   Ⓒ 5   Ⓓ 6

8. Alison is putting stickers in a sticker album. 72 stickers fit on one page. There are 9 stickers in each row. How many rows will there be on one page?

   Ⓐ 7   Ⓑ 6   Ⓒ 8   Ⓓ 10

9. An ice cream shop serves 3 kinds of ice cream, 5 different toppings, and 2 kinds of cones. How many combinations are possible?

   Ⓕ 10   Ⓖ 17   Ⓗ 25   Ⓚ 30

10. Which number completes this function table?

Input	1	2	3	4	5	6
Output	6	12	18	24	30	

   Ⓐ 36   Ⓑ 30   Ⓒ 21   Ⓓ 16

11. What is the rule for this function table?

Distance (d)	1	2	3	4	5
Time (t)	7	14	21	28	35

   Ⓕ $d = 7t$ Ⓖ $t = 6d$ Ⓗ $t = 7d$ Ⓚ $t = 7$

Solve each equation.

12. $5p = 45$

Ⓐ $p = 8$ Ⓑ $p = 9$ Ⓒ $p = 10$ Ⓓ $p = 40$

13. $30 = 10q$

Ⓕ $q = 300$ Ⓖ $q = 20$ Ⓗ $q = 10$ Ⓚ $q = 3$

14. $12 \times 0 = r$

Ⓐ $r = 0$ Ⓑ $r = 1$ Ⓒ $r = 12$ Ⓓ $r = 120$

15. $s = 35 + (15 / 3)$

Ⓕ $s = 30$ Ⓖ $s = 35$ Ⓗ $s = 40$ Ⓚ $s = 45$

Use the Properties of Multiplication to solve for n.

16. $376 \times 1{,}129 = 1{,}129 \times n$

Ⓐ $n = 0$ Ⓑ $n = 1$ Ⓒ $n = 376$ Ⓓ $n = 1{,}129$

17. $(927 \times 285) \times 103 = n \times (285 \times 103)$

Ⓕ $n = 927$ Ⓖ $n = 285$ Ⓗ $n = 103$ Ⓚ $n = 1$

Solve.

18. Bob, Alan, and Joan collect coins. Joan has 12 coins. Alan has twice as many coins as Joan. Bob has 4 times as many coins as Alan. How many coins does Bob have?

    Ⓐ 48 coins   Ⓑ 16 coins   Ⓒ 36 coins   Ⓓ 96 coins

19. Vera and Tomas bought sandwiches for a family picnic for 20 cents each. Tomas bought 27 sandwiches. That is 3 times as many as Vera bought. How much money did Vera spend?

    Ⓕ 100 cents   Ⓖ 180 cents   Ⓗ 27 cents   Ⓚ 20 cents

20. Pam wants to paint 2 walls of her bedroom red. She needs to know the total area of the 2 walls, so the person at the paint store can tell her how much red paint to buy. Both walls are rectangles. One wall is 10 feet tall and 6 feet wide. The other wall is 12 feet tall and 10 feet wide. Which explanation best describes how to solve this problem?

    Ⓐ First multiply 10 • 6 = 60 square feet.
       Then multiply 12 • 10 = 120 square feet.
       Then add 60 + 120 = 180 square feet.

    Ⓑ First add 10 + 6 = 16 square feet.
       Then add 12 + 10 = 22 square feet.
       Then add 16 + 22 = 38 square feet.

    Ⓒ Multiply 10 • 6 • 10 • 12 = 7,200 square feet.

    Ⓓ First multiply 10 • 6 = 60 square feet.
       Then multiply 10 • 12 = 120 square feet.
       Then multiply 60 • 120 = 7,200 square feet.

Multiplication and Division Word Problems

What Is Assessed

- Recall basic multiplication and division.
- Identify and use the properties of multiplication and division.
- Solve one- and two-step problems involving multiplication.

Explaining the Assessment

1. Tell the students that they are going to investigate all the rectangular arrays they can make that will fit in a given area. They could draw a 9 × 10 array of counters to model the classroom area available for desks.

2. Read the activity aloud with the class.

Materials

60 counters for each student, paper

Possible Responses

Question 1: Responses should include multiplication and division sentences for these arrays:

4 × 10 (4 × 10 = 40, 40 ÷ 10 = 4, 40 ÷ 4 = 10)

5 × 8	6 × 7	7 × 6	8 × 5	9 × 5
5 × 9	6 × 8	7 × 7	8 × 6	9 × 6
5 × 10	6 × 9	7 × 8	8 × 7	
	6 × 10			

Question 2: Groups may vary. Students may sort by width or length of array, or by size of product.

Question 3: 16 arrays

Question 4: Strategies may vary. Students may list all arrays with width of 4, then all arrays with width of 5, then 6, and so on.

ACTIVITY Making Arrays

You need to arrange 40 to 60 desks in a classroom. Nine desks fit across the classroom. 10 desks fit from front to back in the classroom. How many ways can you make a rectangular array of desks in this room?

1. On a sheet of paper, make all the arrays you can for multiplying two numbers with a product from 40 to 60. Remember, the columns and rows of desks cannot be longer or wider than the classroom.

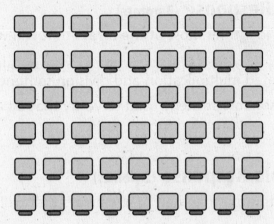

Write a multiplication sentence and a division sentence for each array. Then make the next array.

2. Sort your multiplication sentences for the arrays into groups.

3. How many arrays did you make? _____

4. Explain the strategy you used to find the greatest number of arrays.

_____

_____

_____

Math Expressions   A11
Unit 1 Performance Assessment

Performance Assessment Rubric

An Exemplary Response (4 points)

- Systematically identifies all the arrays that will work for the problem
- Writes all related multiplication and division sentences correctly
- Clearly explains an organized strategy used to verify that all arrays have been found

A Proficient Response (3 points)

- Systematically identifies most of the arrays that will work for the problem
- Writes the related multiplication and division sentences correctly
- Explains a reasonable strategy used to verify that all arrays have been found

An Acceptable Response (2 points)

- Randomly finds more than half of the arrays that will work for the problem
- Does not select any arrays that are too big or too small for the problem
- Writes most related multiplication and division sentences correctly
- Explains why the arrays work for the problem

A Limited Response (1 point)

- Randomly finds some arrays that will work for the problem, and includes some that will not work
- Writes five or more related multiplication and division sentences incorrectly
- Does not explain a strategy for finding or verifying answers

Find the perimeter and area of each rectangle.

1.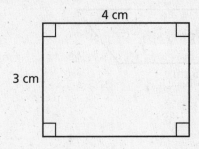

4 cm

3 cm

2.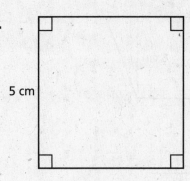

5 cm

P = _____14 cm_____

A = _____12 sq cm_____

P = _____20 cm_____

A = _____25 sq cm_____

Solve.

3. Would you measure the area of a basketball court or the length of a street using square meters? Explain your choice.

Show your work.

area of a basketball court; Possible explanation:

When finding area, the units are always squared.

4. Uli is making a mosaic with special tiles. The tiles are each 1 square centimeter. The mosaic when finished will be 3 meters long and 2 meters wide. How many tiles will Uli need?

_____60,000 tiles_____

5. Hillary is using braided yarn to make a border around a picture frame. The frame is a rectangle with a length of 10 inches and a width of 9 inches. How many inches of braided yarn does she need?

_____38 inches_____

Find the area of each parallelogram.

1.

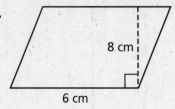

8 cm

6 cm

$A =$ ___48 sq cm___

2.

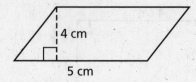

4 cm

5 cm

$A =$ ___20 sq cm___

Find the area of each triangle.

3.

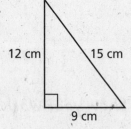

12 cm   15 cm

9 cm

$A =$ ___54 sq cm___

4.

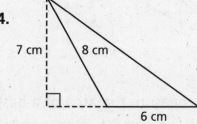

7 cm   8 cm

6 cm

$A =$ ___21 sq cm___

Solve.

5. Matt cut out a paper triangle with a base of 6 cm and a height of 5 cm. What is the area of the triangle?

___15 sq cm___

Show your work.

Name _____   Date _____

Find the perimeter and area.

1.

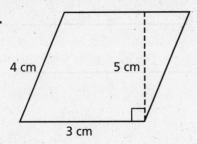

4 cm   5 cm

3 cm

P = _____ 14 cm _____

A = _____ 15 sq cm _____

2.

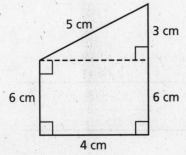

5 cm   3 cm

6 cm   6 cm

4 cm

P = _____ 24 cm _____

A = _____ 30 sq cm _____

Find the perimeter and area of each figure in feet.

3.

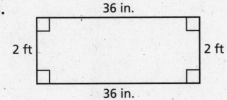

36 in.

2 ft   2 ft

36 in.

P = _____ 10 ft _____

A = _____ 6 sq ft _____

4.

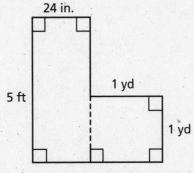

24 in.

5 ft   1 yd

1 yd

P = _____ 20 ft _____

A = _____ 19 sq ft _____

Find the perimeter and area of each figure.

1.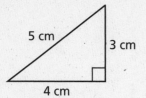

Perimeter _____ 12 cm _____

Area _____ 6 sq cm _____

2.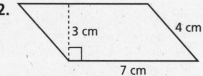

Perimeter _____ 22 cm _____

Area _____ 21 sq cm _____

3.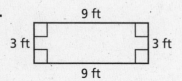

Perimeter _____ 24 ft _____

Area _____ 27 sq ft _____

4.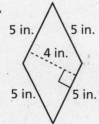

Perimeter _____ 20 in. _____

Area _____ 20 sq in. _____

The rectangular table in Mona's dining room is 6 feet long by 4 feet wide. Solve the problems about the table.

Show your work.

5. Mona wants to make a tablecloth to cover the whole top of the table. How many square feet of cloth does she need?

   24 square feet _____

   _____

6. Mona wants to put a ribbon all the way around the edge of the table. How many feet of ribbon does she need?

   20 feet _____

   _____

Find the perimeter and area of each figure.

7.

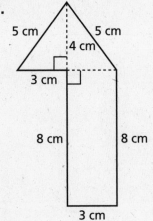

5 cm   5 cm
4 cm
3 cm
8 cm   8 cm
3 cm

8.

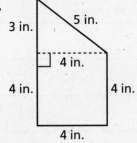

3 in.   5 in.
4 in.
4 in.   4 in.
4 in.

Perimeter _____ 32 cm _____

Area _____ 36 sq cm _____

Perimeter _____ 20 in. _____

Area _____ 22 sq in. _____

A17

Unit 2 Test, Form A

Solve the word problems.

9. A triangle has a base of 48 in. and a height of 3 ft. What is its area in square feet?

   _6 sq ft_____

   _____

10. **Extended Response** Brian is putting a fence around his garden. The garden is 4 feet wide and 7 feet long. He has 10 yd of fence. Does he have enough fence to put a fence all the way around his garden? Explain your answer.

    Yes. The perimeter of the garden is 22 ft. Brian

    has 10 yd or 30 ft of fence. That is enough to go

    around the perimeter of the garden.

    _____

    _____

    _____

    _____

Fill in the circle for the correct answer.

Find the perimeter and area of each figure.

1.

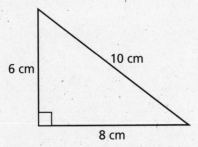

Ⓐ Perimeter = 14 cm; Area = 24 sq cm
Ⓑ Perimeter = 24 cm; Area = 24 sq cm
Ⓒ Perimeter = 24 cm; Area = 48 sq cm
Ⓓ Perimeter = 30 cm; Area = 48 sq cm

2.

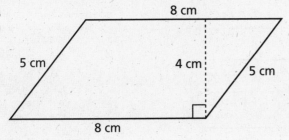

Ⓕ Perimeter = 26 cm; Area = 32 sq cm
Ⓖ Perimeter = 26 cm; Area = 40 sq cm
Ⓗ Perimeter = 32 cm; Area = 26 sq cm
Ⓚ Perimeter = 34 cm; Area = 32 sq cm

3.

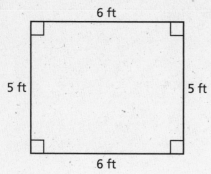

Ⓐ Perimeter = 11 ft; Area = 30 sq ft
Ⓑ Perimeter = 22 ft; Area = 15 sq ft
Ⓒ Perimeter = 22 ft; Area = 30 sq ft
Ⓓ Perimeter = 24 ft; Area = 36 sq ft

4.

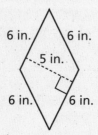

Ⓕ Perimeter = 11 in.; Area = 24 sq in.
Ⓖ Perimeter = 12 in.; Area = 25 sq in.
Ⓗ Perimeter = 18 in.; Area = 36 sq in.
Ⓚ Perimeter = 24 in.; Area = 30 sq in.

The patio in Erika's back yard is 5 yards long by 4 yards wide.
Solve the problems about the patio.

5. Erika's father wants to buy carpeting to cover the whole patio.
How many square yards of carpeting does he need?
Ⓐ 16 square yards
Ⓑ 18 square yards
Ⓒ 20 square yards
Ⓓ 25 square yards

6. Erika's mother wants to put a fence all the way around the patio.
How many yards of fence does she need?
Ⓕ 9 yards
Ⓖ 16 yards
Ⓗ 18 yards
Ⓚ 20 yards

Find the perimeter and area of the figure.

7.

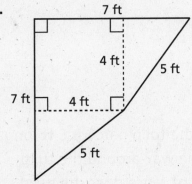

Ⓐ Perimeter = 24 ft; Area = 28 sq ft
Ⓑ Perimeter = 24 ft; Area = 40 sq ft
Ⓒ Perimeter = 28 ft; Area = 24 sq ft
Ⓓ Perimeter = 28 ft; Area = 28 sq ft

Find the perimeter and area of the figure.

8.

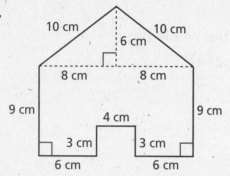

- Ⓕ Perimeter = 54 cm; Area = 180 sq cm
- Ⓖ Perimeter = 60 cm; Area = 180 sq cm
- Ⓗ Perimeter = 60 cm; Area = 192 sq cm
- Ⓚ Perimeter = 82 cm; Area = 180 sq cm

Solve.

9. A rectangle is 3 ft long and 24 in. wide. What is its area in square feet?
   - Ⓐ 5 sq ft
   - Ⓑ 6 sq ft
   - Ⓒ 10 sq ft
   - Ⓓ 72 sq ft

10. The tulip patch in a park is a rhombus. One side of the tulip patch is 6 ft long. The gardener at the park wants to put a fence all the way around the tulip patch. She has 7 yd of fence. How many more yards of fence does she need to be able to put a fence all the way around the tulip patch? (Remember 1 yd = 3 ft.)
    - Ⓕ 1 yard
    - Ⓖ 2 yards
    - Ⓗ 3 yards
    - Ⓚ 4 yards

Perimeter and Area

What Is Assessed
- Find perimeter and area of polygons.
- Use metric measurements to solve problems involving perimeter and area.
- Find perimeter and area of complex figures.

Explaining the Assessment

1. Tell the students that they are going to make special figures called pentominos by attaching 5 squares together. All their pentominos must be different.

   Explain that these two pentominos are identical because you can flip one onto the other.

2. Read the activity aloud with the class.

Materials
Centimeter-grid paper

Possible Responses
Question 1:

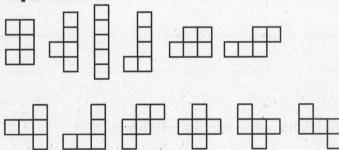

Question 2: There are 12 different pentominos.

Question 3: Every pentomino is made up of 5 squares. Each square is 1 sq cm in area. So every pentomino is 5 sq cm in area.

Question 4: All but one of pentominos have a perimeter of 12 cm. This one has a perimeter of 10 cm. It has more interior edges that are not part of the perimeter.

ACTIVITY Pentominos

A *pentomino* is a rectangle or complex figure
made up of 5 attached squares.

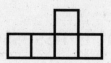

1. Draw as many different pentominos as you can
   on centimeter-grid paper.

   If you can flip or turn a pentomino to match
   another pentomino, then the two pentominos
   are not different.

2. How many different pentominos did you find?

   _____

3. Do all pentominos have the same area?
   Explain.

   _____

   _____

   _____

   _____

4. Do all pentominos have the same perimeter?

   Explain.

   _____

   _____

   _____

Performance Assessment Rubric

An Exemplary Response (4 points)

- Draws all 12 different pentominos
- Clearly explains why the areas are all the same
- Identifies the pentomino with a different perimeter and clearly explains why it is different

A Proficient Response (3 points)

- Draws at least 10 different pentominos with no duplicates
- Clearly explains why the areas are all the same
- May not draw the one pentomino with a different perimeter

An Acceptable Response (2 points)

- Draws at least 8 different pentominos; may have some duplicates
- Explains why the areas are all the same
- May not draw or identify the one pentomino with a different perimeter

A Limited Response (1 point)

- Draws fewer than 8 different pentominos; may have some duplicates
- May not be able to explain that the areas are the same, or explain why
- May not draw or identify the one pentomino with a different perimeter

Lesson 1-4

Write the decimal number.

1. eight hundred forty-three thousandths ___0.843___

Compare. Write > (greater than) or < (less than).

2. 0.913 ⟨ < ⟩ 0.931

3. 7.8 ⟨ > ⟩ 7.08

Write these decimals in order from least to greatest.

4. 1.01   0.09   0.10   2.00   0.01

___0.01___ ___0.09___ ___0.10___ ___1.01___ ___2.00___

Add and subtract the pair of decimal numbers.

5. 0.654 and 0.32   sum: ___0.974___   difference: ___0.334___

Write the decimal number.

1. one billion, seven hundred twenty-six million, nine hundred fourteen thousand, seven hundred two and five billionths

   1,726,914,702.000000005

Compare. Write > (greater than) or < (less than).

2. 6,235,901,410 (<) 6,235,901,420

Follow the directions to change the number in the box. 498,763.06

3. Write a number with 8 more in the tens place. 498,843.06

4. Decrease the number by 3 tenths. 498,762.76

5. Increase the number by 10,000. 508,763.06

Lesson 7-11

Name _____ Date _____

Add each pair of numbers.

1. 23,841 + 32,064 = __55,905__

2. 384,071.2 + 20,517.89 = __404,589.09__

Subtract each pair of numbers.

3. 50,000 − 23,901 = __26,099__

4. 629,813.2 − 201,697.65 = __428,115.55__

Group the numbers to make the addition easier.

5.   11.7
       11.55
       11.3
      11.45
   + 11.65
       57.65

Unit 3
Quick Quiz 4

Name

Date

lesson
12-17

1. Round 7,451.348 to the nearest hundred.
   Then, round 7,451.348 to the nearest tenth.

   _7,500; 7,451.3_

Use the pictograph to answer the question.

2. How many more girls than boys went to
   the soccer game?

   20 more girls

Students Attending Soccer Game

Boys	👤 👤 👤 👤
Girls	👤 👤 👤 👤 👤 👤

👤 = 10 students

Use the bar graph to answer each question.

3. The graph shows the number of
   people who went to a carnival.
   How many people went to the
   carnival in all?

   1,100 people

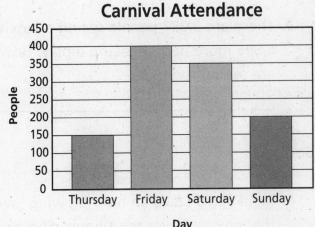

Carnival Attendance

4. How many more people went on
   Friday than went on Thursday?

   250 people

Use the line graph to answer each question.

5. Between which two weeks did the flower
   grow the least amount?

   between weeks 3 and 4

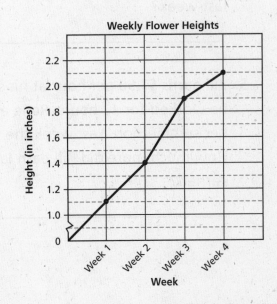

Weekly Flower Heights

Lesson 18-21

Write an equation for each problem, then solve the problem. *Show your work.*

1. A factory made 39,467 bolts in January. The factory made some more bolts in February. The factory made 62,011 bolts altogether in January and February. How many bolts did the factory make in February?

   $39,467 + b = 62,011; 22,544$ bolts

2. A school's students collected 50,000 cans to recycle. They took 32,579 of them to the recycling center. How many cans do they have left?

   $50,000 - 32,579 = c; 17,421$

3. There are 2,387 people seeing a movie. There are 5,896 more people seeing a play. How many people are seeing the play?

   $2,387 + 5,896 = p; 8,283$ people

Solve.

4. Rene earns $8.00 an hour mowing lawns. Last week she mowed lawns for 4 hours. She also earned $15.00 washing cars last week. How much did she earn last week?

   $47.00

5. Bill earns $7.50 per hour at his summer job. Last week he worked for 12 hours. Rene earns $6.75 per hour at her summer job. Last week she worked for 10 hours. How much more did Bill earn last week than Rene earned?

   $22.50

Write each number.

1. thirty-seven thousand,
   five hundred sixty ___37,560___

2. three million, six hundred two thousand,
   eight hundred twenty-four ___3,602,824___

3. seven tenths ___0.7___

4. five hundred twenty-eight thousandths
   ___0.528___

Compare. Write > (greater than) or < (less than).

5. 789,261 (<) 798,612

6. 3,491,652 (>) 3,419,652

7. 0.741 (>) 0.714

8. 0.08 (<) 0.6

Add or subtract each pair of numbers. Then show how to estimate to check your answer.

9. 652,721 + 201,054 = ___853,775___

10. 1.392 + 0.85 = ___2.242___

11. 794,627 − 322,069 = ___472,558___

12. 6.418 − 1.37 = ___5.048___

Use the pictograph to answer each question.

13. How many birds are on
    the farm? ___140 birds___

14. How many more ducks
    than chickens are there
    on the farm? ___40 more ducks___

Birds on a Farm

= 10 birds

Use the bar graph to answer each question.

15. The graph shows the number of
    people at each basketball game
    last week. How many people saw
    a basketball game last week?
    ___900 people___

16. How many more people went to
    Game 2 than went to Game 1?
    ___150 people___

Attendance at Basketball Games

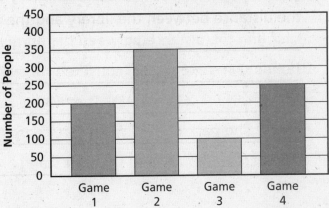

Use the line graph to answer each question.

17. The graph shows the number of cats that needed homes at the end of each year. What was the number of cats that needed homes at the end of 2004?

_____60 cats_____

18. How many more cats needed homes at the end of 2003 than at the end of 2004? _____10 cats_____

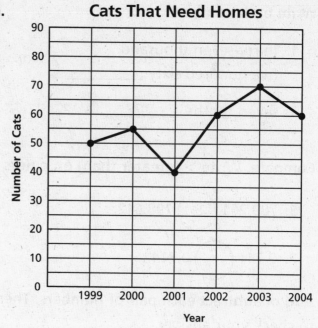

Cats That Need Homes

Solve.   *Show your work.*

19. Eliza is serving nuts for a snack. She plans to mix 1.2 pounds of almonds and 0.75 pounds of cashews. How many pounds of nuts is that altogether?

1.95 pounds

_____

20. Extended Response The distance between the library and the park is 1,563 feet. The distance between the library and the bank is 528 feet. The distance between the library and the fruit stand is 296 feet less than the distance between the library and the bank. Explain how to find how much greater the distance between the library and the park is than the distance between the library and the fruit stand.

First find the distance between the library and the fruit

stand, 528 − 296 = 232 feet. Then subtract the distance from

1,563, 1,563 − 232 = 1,331. The distance between the

library and park is 1,331 feet more than the distance

between the library and the fruit stand.

Fill in the circle for the correct answer.

Choose the correct standard form for each number.

1. sixty-two thousand, five hundred nine

   Ⓐ 26,509   Ⓑ 62,509   Ⓒ 62,590   Ⓓ 62,905

2. eight million, four hundred twenty thousand, six hundred thirty-seven

   Ⓕ 8,000   Ⓖ 8,240   Ⓗ 8,240,637   Ⓚ 8,420,637

3. six hundredths

   Ⓐ 0.06   Ⓑ 0.006   Ⓒ 0.0006   Ⓓ 0.00006

4. nine hundred forty-five thousandths

   Ⓕ 0.0945   Ⓖ 0.459   Ⓗ 0.945   Ⓚ 945

Compare. What symbol makes each true?

5. 867,277 ◯ 876,722   6. 3,264,620 ◯ 3,624,620

   Ⓐ >   Ⓑ <   Ⓒ =   Ⓕ >   Ⓖ <   Ⓗ =

7. 0.041 ◯ 0.140   8. 0.747 ◯ 0.724

   Ⓐ >   Ⓑ <   Ⓒ =   Ⓕ >   Ⓖ <   Ⓗ =

Add or subtract.

9. 238,721 + 401,566

   Ⓐ 640,187   Ⓑ 640,287   Ⓒ 641,287   Ⓓ 740,287

10. 0.67 + 1.038

   Ⓕ 1.708   Ⓖ 1.608   Ⓗ 0.708   Ⓚ 0.1708

11. 752,828 − 301,652

   Ⓐ 454,176   Ⓑ 452,176   Ⓒ 451,176   Ⓓ 451,175

12. 6.872 − 1.53

   Ⓕ 54.42   Ⓖ 53.42   Ⓗ 5.442   Ⓚ 5.342

Use the pictograph to answer each question.

13. How many students take painting class?

   Ⓐ 120 students   Ⓑ 130 students
   Ⓒ 140 students   Ⓓ 150 students

14. How many fewer girls than boys take painting class?

   Ⓕ 20 fewer   Ⓖ 30 fewer
   Ⓗ 40 fewer   Ⓚ 50 fewer

Students Taking Painting Class

= 10 students

Use the bar graph to answer each question.

15. The graph shows the number of apples sold at a fruit stand each day. How many apples were sold for the four days?

    Ⓐ 800 apples   Ⓑ 850 apples
    Ⓒ 900 apples   Ⓓ 950 apples

16. How many more apples were sold on Thursday than on Wednesday?

    Ⓕ 150 apples   Ⓖ 140 apples
    Ⓗ 130 apples   Ⓚ 120 apples

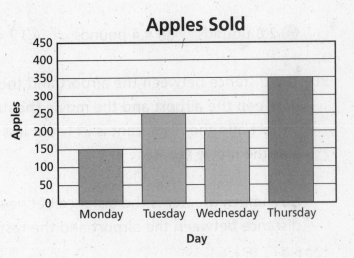

Use the line graph to answer each question.

17. The graph shows the number of eagles spotted at a park each year. How many eagles were spotted in 2000?

    Ⓐ 60 eagles   Ⓑ 70 eagles
    Ⓒ 80 eagles   Ⓓ 90 eagles

18. How many fewer eagles were spotted in 2001 than in 2000?

    Ⓕ 10 eagles   Ⓖ 15 eagles
    Ⓗ 20 eagles   Ⓚ 25 eagles

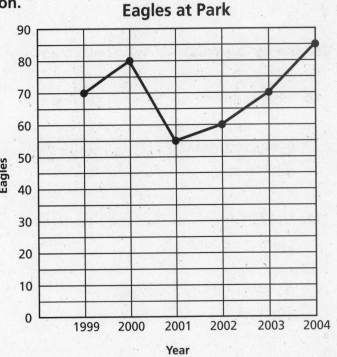

Math Expressions
A35
Unit 3 Test, Form B

Solve.

19. A 7-month old panda bear weighs 12.4 kilograms. At 5 months, she weighed 9.6 kilograms. How much weight did she gain?

    Ⓐ 2.8 pounds   Ⓑ 4.4 pounds   Ⓒ 7.4 pounds   Ⓓ 13.6 pounds

20. The distance between the airport and the hotel is 1,304 feet. The distance between the airport and the movie theater is 432 feet. The distance between the airport and the restaurant is 211 feet less than the distance between the airport and the movie theater.

    How much greater is the distance between the airport and the hotel than the distance between the airport and the restaurant?

    Ⓕ 211 feet   Ⓖ 1,525 feet   Ⓗ 643 feet   Ⓚ 1,083 feet

Math Expressions
A36
Unit 3 Test, Form B

Addition and Subtraction With Whole Numbers and Decimals

What Is Assessed

- Read, write, and identify the place value of decimals and whole numbers.
- Add and subtract whole numbers and decimals.
- Solve a variety of problems involving addition and subtraction of whole numbers and decimals.

Explaining the Assessment

1. Tell the students that they will be creating a magic square in which all of the rows, columns, and diagonals have the same sum. Explain that they will need to test numbers to see if they work and then make changes to their work if necessary.

2. Read the activity aloud with the class.

Possible Responses

Question 1: 340

Question 2:

160	30	20	130
50	100	110	80
90	60	70	120
40	150	140	10

1.6	0.3	0.2	1.3
0.5	1	1.1	0.8
0.9	0.6	0.7	1.2
0.4	1.5	1.4	0.1

Question 3: Check students' explanations. They may explain that numbers that showed hundreds, tens, and ones have been changed to numbers that show ones, tenths, and hundredths. Each number is now $\frac{1}{100}$ the size of the original number.

Question 4: Students can use any number to add to, subtract from, or multiply or divide by to change every number in the square.

ACTIVITY **Magic Squares**

This square is called "magic" because every row, column, and diagonal add up to the same number. That number is called the *magic sum*.

1. What is the magic sum for this

   magic square? _____

160	30	20	130
50		110	
	60	70	
			10

2. Fill in the missing numbers in the magic square.

3. Show how you could use the first magic square to make a new one with a magic sum of 3.4. Explain why this will work.

   _____

   _____

   _____

   _____

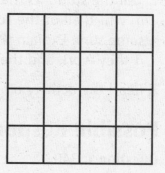

4. Use one of the first two magic squares to make your own magic square with a different magic sum from the first two. Test your magic square. Explain how you created your square.

   _____

   _____

   _____

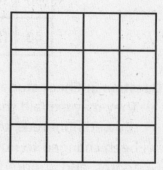

Performance Assessment Rubric

An Exemplary Response (4 points)

- Completes all puzzles without computational errors
- Using place-value concepts, explains why you can change the decimal point in each number and the square will still be magic
- Clearly explains the strategy used to create a new magic square; the strategy may contain complex operations or series of operations

A Proficient Response (3 points)

- Completes the first two puzzles without computational errors
- Explains that changing the magic sum means changing every number in the square the same way, such as dividing each number by 100
- Clearly explains the strategy used to create a new magic square

An Acceptable Response (2 points)

- Completes the first two puzzles with few computational errors
- Shows some understanding that changing the magic sum means changing every number in the square the same way
- Explains a simple strategy used to create a new magic square

A Limited Response (1 point)

- Completes the first puzzle with some computational errors
- Does not apply the concepts of multiplication or place value to create the second puzzle
- Does not create a new magic square that works

1. Measure each angle with your protractor. Write the measure.
   Then, decide if the angles are *complementary*, *supplementary*, or
   neither.

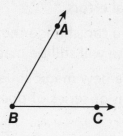
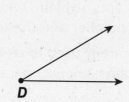

∠ABC = __60°__   ∠D = __30°__

The two angles are __complementary__ .

2. Name two pairs of vertical angles.

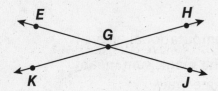

∠EGH and ∠KGJ

∠EGK and ∠HGJ

Write the measure of the unknown angle.

3.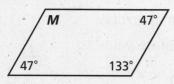

   __133°__

4.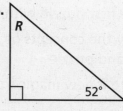

   __38°__

5. Draw a figure that is congruent to the figure below.

   Answers will vary. Possible answer:

1. The measure of the shaded region is given. Write the measure of the angle that is not shaded.

___275°___

2. Decide if the figure has line symmetry and rotational symmetry. If the figure has line symmetry, draw the line(s) of symmetry. If the figure has rotational symmetry, give the degrees of the rotational symmetry. Explain your answers.

This figure has one vertical line of symmetry and no rotational symmetry, because it does not look the same until it is returned to its original position.

3. The circle graph represents a survey of students. The students were asked to name their favorite school subject. Of the students surveyed, 50 voted for math. How many students were surveyed?

Favorite Subject

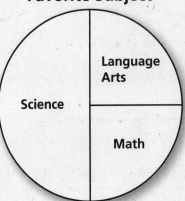

___200 students; 50 + 50 + 2(50) = 200___

Solve. Use 3 for π.

4. The circumference of a circle is 27 inches. About how long is a diameter of that circle?

___about 9 inches___

5. The circumference of a circle is 60 inches. About how long is a radius of that circle?

___about 10 inches___

Use these angles to answer questions 1 and 2.

1. Name the pair of supplementary angles.

   ∠STV and ∠VTU

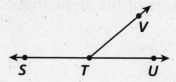

2. Name the straight angle.

   ∠STU

Write the measure of the unknown angle.

3.

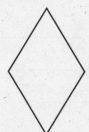

   50°

4.

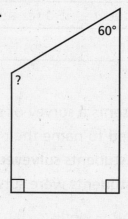

   120°

5. Circle all the polygons that look congruent to each other.

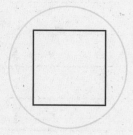  

6. Draw the figure after a counter-clockwise turn of 90°.

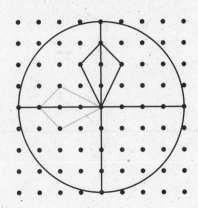

7. Draw all of the lines of symmetry for the hexagon.

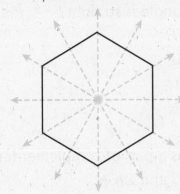

Use the circle graph to answer questions 8–10.

8. Which color did most people prefer?

_____Red_____

9. What color was preferred by the least number of people?

_____Yellow_____

Preferred Color

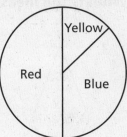

10. **Extended Response** 153 people preferred red. 105 people preferred blue. How many people preferred yellow? Explain your answer.

48 people. It looks like the same number of people preferred red as did yellow and blue combined. Because 105 + 48 = 153, 48 preferred yellow.

_____

_____

_____

Fill in the circle for the correct answer.

Use these angles to answer questions 1 and 2.

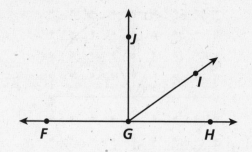

1. Which angle is straight?

    Ⓐ ∠FGH

    Ⓑ ∠FGJ

    Ⓒ ∠JGI

    Ⓓ ∠JGH

2. Which is a pair of complementary angles?

    Ⓕ ∠FGJ and ∠IGH

    Ⓖ ∠FGJ and ∠JGH

    Ⓗ ∠JGI and ∠IGH

    Ⓚ ∠JGI and ∠JGH

What is the measure of the unknown angle?

3.

    Ⓐ 45°

    Ⓑ 135°

    Ⓒ 180°

    Ⓓ 360°

4.

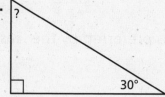

    Ⓕ 180°

    Ⓖ 150°

    Ⓗ 90°

    Ⓚ 60°

5. Which of these polygons are congruent?

    Ⓐ A and B

    Ⓑ C and D

    Ⓒ B and E

    Ⓓ A and E

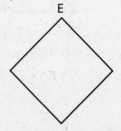

Use this arrow to answer question 6. The arrow points right.

6. This arrow will point left after a
   Ⓕ 360° turn counter-clockwise.
   Ⓖ 180° turn clockwise.
   Ⓗ 90° turn clockwise.
   Ⓚ 90° turn counter-clockwise.

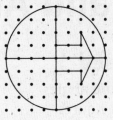

7. This figure has
   Ⓐ no lines of symmetry.
   Ⓑ one line of symmetry.
   Ⓒ two lines of symmetry.
   Ⓓ four lines of symmetry.

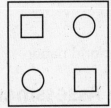

Use the circle graph to answer questions 8–10.

8. Which fruit did most people prefer?
   Ⓕ apples
   Ⓖ bananas
   Ⓗ grapes
   Ⓚ oranges

Preferred Fruit

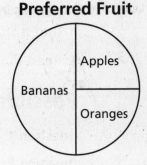

9. Which fruit was preferred by the same number of people who preferred oranges?
   Ⓐ apples
   Ⓑ bananas
   Ⓒ grapes
   Ⓓ oranges

10. In the survey, 15 people preferred apples. How many people were in the survey?
    Ⓕ 15 people
    Ⓖ 30 people
    Ⓗ 45 people
    Ⓚ 60 people

Math Expressions
A45
Unit 4 Test, Form B

Circles, Polygons, and Angles

What Is Assessed

- Identify and measure angles.
- Identify congruent figures.
- Identify the position of an object after it has been turned.
- Identify lines of symmetry.

Materials

Protractor, centimeter-grid paper

Explaining the Assessment

1. To introduce the activity tasks, draw a circle on the board divided into six pieces. Explain that students will apply the knowledge they have gained in this unit to make conclusions about a large wheel of cheese that a store is cutting up in a similar manner.

2. Read the task aloud with the class.

Possible Responses

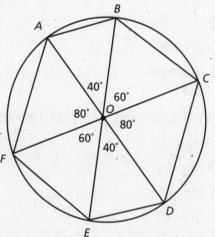

Question 1: 3 cuts

Question 2: a hexagon

Question 3: Triangles *AOB* and *EOD*
Triangles *AOF* and *COD*
Triangles *FOE* and *BOC*

These pairs of triangles have matching sides of equal length.

Question 4: Turn a triangle about *O* until it fits over the opposite triangle (or reflect the triangle in a diameter of the circle).

Question 5: lines *AD, FC,* or *BE*

Question 6: The total is 360°.

Question 7: The angles around the center form two straight angles on any of the lines of symmetry. So the total is 2 × 180° = 360°.

Name _____   Date _____

ACTIVITY The Big Cheese

. . . .

Bob's Cheese Mart is dividing up a large, round piece of cheese into six pieces. Each cut of the cheese forms a diameter through the center.

1. Draw diameters to divide Bob's cheese into 6 pieces. How many cuts did you have to make?

   _____

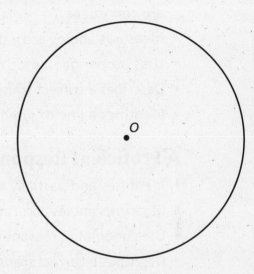

2. Label the six points on the edge of the cheese, *A, B, C, D, E,* and *F.* Join the points around the circle. What polygon did you make?

   _____

3. Name two congruent triangles. Why are they congruent?

   _____   _____

   _____

4. How could you transform one of the congruent triangles into the other?

   _____

5. Name a line of symmetry of the circle. _____

   _____

6. Measure and label the 6 angles at the center of the cheese. What is the

   total measure of the angles? _____

7. Explain how you could know the sum of the angles without adding.

   _____

   _____

                                                      Unit 4 Performance Assessment

Performance Assessment Rubric

An Exemplary Response (4 points)

- Identifies congruent triangles and clearly explains why the triangles are congruent
- Measures angles accurately (to nearest degree)
- Uses proper geometric reasoning efficiently to solve problems
- Describes a correct transformation
- Identifies a line of symmetry and the interior angle of a circle

A Proficient Response (3 points)

- Identifies and partially explains why triangles are congruent
- Measures angles accurately (to nearest 2 degrees)
- Uses geometric reasoning to solve problems
- Describes a correct transformation
- Identifies a line of symmetry and the interior angle of a circle

An Acceptable Response (2 points)

- Partially explains why triangles are congruent
- Measures angles within 10°
- May use incorrect reasoning to solve problems
- May describe an incorrect transformation
- May identify a line of symmetry and/or the interior angle of a circle

A Limited Response (1 point)

- May not identify congruent triangles or explain why triangles are congruent
- Measures angles inaccurately
- May use incorrect reasoning to solve problems
- May not describe a transformation
- May not identify a line of symmetry and/or the interior angle of a circle

Add or subtract.

1. $\frac{3}{7} + \frac{2}{7} =$ ___ $\frac{5}{7}$

2. $\frac{3}{4} - \frac{2}{4} =$ ___ $\frac{1}{4}$

3. Circle the greater fraction. Then write the correct sign (> or <) between them.

$\left(\frac{1}{5}\right) > \frac{1}{7}$

4. Fill in the correct fraction.

$\frac{3}{7} +$ ___ $\frac{4}{7}$ $= 1$

5. Name the fraction that represents each shaded part. Explain what each fraction represents.

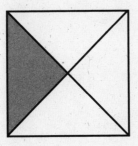

$\frac{1}{4}$

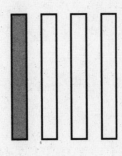

$\frac{1}{4}$

Sample. The first fraction represents 1 of 4 equal pieces of the whole.

The second fraction represents 1 bar of the group of 4 equal bars.

1. Write the mixed number as an improper fraction.

$6\frac{3}{8}$ = $\frac{51}{8}$

2. Write the improper fraction as a mixed number.

$\frac{13}{4}$ = $3\frac{1}{4}$

Add or subtract.

3. $\frac{5}{9} + \frac{7}{9}$ = $1\frac{3}{9}$ or $1\frac{1}{3}$

4. $5\frac{3}{4} + 5\frac{3}{4}$ = $11\frac{2}{4}$ or $11\frac{1}{2}$

5. $7\frac{1}{6} - 3\frac{5}{6}$ = $3\frac{2}{6}$ or $3\frac{1}{3}$

Add or subtract. Simplify your answers.

1. $3\frac{5}{6} + 4\frac{2}{3} =$ ___$8\frac{1}{2}$___

2. $5\frac{1}{3} - 1\frac{5}{9} =$ ___$3\frac{7}{9}$___

3. Circle the equivalent fraction.

$\frac{5}{9} =$ $\frac{12}{18}$ $\left(\frac{15}{27}\right)$ $\frac{20}{54}$

Solve. Simplify your answer if possible.   *Show your work.*

4. Ann has 6 red cubes and 2 blue cubes in a box. She
reaches in and chooses one without looking. What is
the probability that it is a blue cube? Simplify your
answer if possible.

   ___$\frac{1}{4}$___

5. Jen rides the bus for $\frac{2}{3}$ of an hour before she gets off.
Amy gets off the bus $\frac{1}{5}$ of an hour after Jen does.
What is the total length of Amy's ride on the bus?

   ___$\frac{13}{15}$ of an hour___

Write the equivalent decimal form.

1. $\frac{4}{5}$ __0.8__

2. $\frac{3}{4}$ __0.75__

3. Compare. Write >, <, or =.

   $0.834 \left(>\right) \frac{5}{6}$

4. Write the numbers in order from least to greatest.

   $5\frac{7}{10}$ $\frac{7}{8}$ 0.87 5.3 $\frac{28}{5}$ __0.87; $\frac{7}{8}$; 5.3; $\frac{28}{5}$, $5\frac{7}{10}$__

5. Estimate by rounding each number to the nearest whole number. Then add.

   $4\frac{3}{7} + 2\frac{9}{16}$

   Estimate: __7__

Name _____   Date _____

Add or subtract. Simplify your answers.

1. a. $\frac{2}{5} + \frac{1}{5} =$ ___ $\frac{3}{5}$ b. $\frac{5}{6} - \frac{1}{3} =$ ___ $\frac{1}{2}$

2. a.
$$5\frac{3}{8}$$
$$-\ 4\frac{5}{8}$$
$$\overline{\quad\frac{3}{4}\quad}$$

b.
$$2\frac{3}{4}$$
$$+\ 3\frac{1}{8}$$
$$\overline{\quad 5\frac{7}{8}\quad}$$

3. Find s.

$\frac{1}{s} + \frac{1}{s} + \frac{1}{s} + \frac{1}{s} = \frac{5}{5}$ $s =$ ___ 4

4. Circle the greater fraction. Then write $>$ or $<$ between the fractions. Explain your thinking.

$\frac{3}{8}$ $\left(<\right)$ $\left(\frac{3}{7}\right)$

Sevenths are larger than eighths since it takes fewer of them to make a whole. Each fraction has a numerator of three, so three sevenths is greater.

5. Write the mixed number as an improper fraction. Show your work.

$3\frac{1}{3} =$ ___ $\frac{10}{3}$ $3\frac{1}{3} = 1 + 1 + 1 + \frac{1}{3} = \frac{3}{3} + \frac{3}{3} + \frac{3}{3} + \frac{1}{3} = \frac{10}{3}$

6. Write these fractions in order from **least to greatest**.

$\frac{11}{12}$, $1\frac{2}{12}$, $\frac{2}{3}$, $\frac{8}{6}$, $\frac{3}{3}$

$\frac{2}{3}$, $\frac{11}{12}$, $\frac{3}{3}$, $1\frac{2}{12}$, $\frac{8}{6}$

7. Write these numbers in order from **greatest to least**.

$\frac{10}{5}$, 2.02, $\frac{1,000}{1,000}$, $2\frac{1}{10}$, $\frac{4}{5}$

$2\frac{1}{10}$, 2.02, $\frac{10}{5}$, $\frac{1,000}{1,000}$, $\frac{4}{5}$

8. Circle the fraction that is equivalent to $\frac{3}{5}$. Show your work.

$\frac{33}{50}$ $\left(\frac{12}{20}\right)$ $\frac{15}{35}$ $\frac{3}{5} \times \frac{4}{4} = \frac{12}{20}$

Solve. Simplify your answer.

Show your work.

9. Kellen has 5 red marbles and 10 yellow marbles in a bag. He reaches in and chooses one without looking. What is the probability that it is a red marble?

$\frac{1}{3}$

10. **Extended Response** Kim played in the park for $\frac{2}{3}$ hours. Later, Simone played for $\frac{1}{5}$ hours more than Kim. How many hours did they play altogether?

First calculate how long Simone played by adding

both fractions together: $\frac{2}{3} + \frac{1}{5} = \frac{13}{15}$ Then add the

amount of time that Kim played to the amount of

time that Simone played: $\frac{13}{15} + \frac{2}{3} = 1\frac{8}{15}$ Together

they played for $1\frac{8}{15}$ hours.

Fill in the circle for the correct answer.

Add or subtract. Simplify your answers.

1. $\frac{2}{7} + \frac{3}{7} =$

   (A) $\frac{5}{14}$　　　(B) $\frac{5}{7}$　　　(C) $\frac{6}{7}$　　　(D) $1\frac{3}{7}$

2. $\frac{4}{5} - \frac{3}{10} =$

   (F) $\frac{1}{15}$　　　(G) $\frac{1}{10}$　　　(H) $\frac{1}{2}$　　　(K) $\frac{7}{10}$

3. 　$6\frac{1}{6}$
   $-\ 3\frac{1}{3}$

   (A) $2\frac{5}{6}$　　　(B) 3　　　(C) $3\frac{1}{9}$　　　(D) $3\frac{1}{6}$

4. Find n.

   $\frac{1}{n} + \frac{1}{n} + \frac{1}{n} = \frac{n}{n}$

   (F) 1　　　(G) 3　　　(H) 9　　　(K) 6

5. Choose the greatest fraction.

   (A) $\frac{4}{9}$　　　(B) $\frac{4}{10}$　　　(C) $\frac{4}{11}$　　　(D) $\frac{4}{12}$

6. Choose the improper fraction that correctly completes the equation.

$$2\frac{4}{5} =$$

(F) $\frac{12}{5}$　　　　(G) $\frac{14}{5}$　　　　(H) $\frac{14}{4}$　　　　(K) $\frac{24}{5}$

7. Which set of numbers are written in order from least to greatest?

(A) $\frac{8}{2}, \frac{3}{4}, \frac{8}{8}, 2\frac{3}{16}$

(B) $\frac{8}{2}, 2\frac{3}{16}, \frac{8}{8}, \frac{3}{4}$

(C) $\frac{3}{4}, \frac{8}{8}, 2\frac{3}{16}, \frac{8}{2}$

(D) $\frac{8}{8}, 2\frac{3}{16}, \frac{3}{4}, \frac{8}{2}$

8. Which fraction is equivalent to $\frac{4}{7}$?

(F) $\frac{8}{21}$　　　　(G) $\frac{20}{35}$　　　　(H) $\frac{8}{12}$　　　　(K) $\frac{7}{4}$

Solve.

9. Miami has 4 red pencils and 2 yellow pencils in her bag. She reaches in and chooses one without looking. What is the probability that it is a yellow pencil?

(A) $\frac{1}{4}$　　　　(B) $\frac{1}{3}$　　　　(C) $\frac{1}{2}$　　　　(D) $\frac{2}{3}$

10. Peyton read for $\frac{3}{4}$ of an hour. Allison read for $\frac{4}{5}$ of an hour more than Peyton. How many hours did they read altogether?

(F) $\frac{7}{9}$　　　　(G) $1\frac{3}{5}$　　　　(H) $2\frac{1}{5}$　　　　(K) $2\frac{3}{10}$

Math Expressions

A56

Unit 5 Test, Form B

Addition and Subtraction with Fractions

What Is Assessed
- Add and subtract fractions with like and unlike denominators.
- Write and compare fractions.
- Find equivalent fractions.
- Solve problems involving fractions.

Explaining the Assessment

1. To introduce the activity tasks, talk with students about how fractions are used to show the results of surveys and make comparisons about the popularity of consumer items.

2. Read the activity aloud with the class.

Possible Responses

Question 1: Students need to find the sum of the 3 fractions and then find a fourth fraction that will make one whole.

$$\frac{1}{6} + \frac{1}{3} + \frac{2}{5} = \frac{5}{30} + \frac{10}{30} + \frac{12}{30} = \frac{27}{30}$$

$$1 - \frac{27}{30} = \frac{3}{30} = \frac{1}{10}$$

Question 2:

$$\frac{1}{4} + \frac{1}{10} + \frac{3}{10} + \frac{3}{20} + \frac{1}{20} = \frac{5}{20} + \frac{2}{20} + \frac{6}{20} + \frac{3}{20} + \frac{1}{20} = \frac{17}{20}$$

$$1 - \frac{17}{20} = \frac{3}{20}$$

Question 3: Answers will vary but they should show a sense of the order of popularity of the shirts. The fractions should also add to 1.

Name _____   Date _____

ACTIVITY Sports Jersey Sales

Suppose your family has a store that sells sports jerseys.
You need to decide what types of jerseys to order for
next year to stock the store shelves.

This table shows what customers say they may be looking to buy.

Type of jersey	baseball	basketball	hockey	soccer
Fraction	$\frac{2}{5}$	$\frac{1}{3}$		$\frac{1}{6}$

Color	white	red	green	blue	black	other
Fraction	$\frac{1}{4}$	$\frac{1}{10}$		$\frac{3}{10}$	$\frac{3}{20}$	$\frac{1}{20}$

1. What fraction of customers might buy a hockey jersey?
   Explain your answer.

   _____

   _____

2. What fraction of customers like green jerseys?
   Explain your answer.

   _____

   _____

3. Suppose your family decides to order only 5 combinations of jerseys and colors, for
   example, white soccer jerseys. Write the 5 combinations and decide what fraction of
   your store's order should be used for each type of jersey.

Jersey					
Fraction					

   Explain how you decided on your fractions.

   _____

Unit 5 Performance Assessment

Performance Assessment Rubric

An Exemplary Response (4 points)

- Determines equivalent fractions and adds correctly
- Subtracts from 1 to find the missing fractions
- Chooses reasonable fractions for the shirt order and explains answers clearly
- Uses fractions that add to 1

A Proficient Response (3 points)

- Determines equivalent fractions and adds correctly
- Subtracts from 1 to find the missing fractions
- Chooses mostly reasonable fractions for the shirt order
- Uses fractions that add to 1

An Acceptable Response (2 points)

- Determines equivalent fractions but makes some errors in calculations
- Subtracts from 1 to find the missing fractions
- Chooses some reasonable fractions for the shirt order
- May not use fractions that add to 1

A Limited Response (1 point)

- Makes errors in calculations
- May not subtract from 1 to find the missing fractions
- Chooses unreasonable fractions for the shirt order
- May not use fractions that add to 1

For each question, write whether you would measure for *length*, *area*, or *volume*.

1. The amount of space inside of a box _____ volume _____

2. The amount of wallpaper needed to cover a wall _____ area _____

Solve.

Show your work.

3. A cabinet has a volume of 30 cubic feet. The cabinet is 3 feet long and 2 feet wide. How deep is it?

   _____ 5 feet _____

4. The base of the sandbox is 24 square feet. A new sandbox is being built in the park that is twice as long and twice as wide. What will be the area of the new sandbox?

   _____ 96 square feet _____

5. Amanda bought a box with a volume of 10 cubic inches. She then bought another box that is twice as long, twice as wide, and twice as deep. What is the volume of the new box?

   _____ 80 cubic inches _____

Solve.

Show your work.

1. What fraction of 1 quart is 1 cup? $\frac{1}{4}$

2. Kayla was shipping 4 boxes. Three of the boxes each weighed 1 kilogram and the fourth box weighed 750 grams. Altogether, how many grams did the shipment weigh?

   3,750 g

3. A snack mix is sold as 40¢ per ounce. How much will it cost to buy 1.5 pounds of the snack mix?

   $9.60

Add or subtract.

4.　　　4 kg
　　　– 2 kg 100 g

　　　1 kg 900 g

5.　　　3 gal 2 qt
　　　+ 1 gal 3 qt

　　　5 gal 1 qt

Solve.

Show your work.

1. The low temperature of the day was −3°F. The high temperature of the day was 23° higher. What was the high temperature of the day?

   _____20°F_____

2. The 5 A.M. temperature was −9°C. The 5 P.M. temperature was 4°C. How many degrees did the temperature change from 5 P.M. to 5 A.M.? Was the change an increase or a decrease?

   _____13°; increase_____

3. A city tour is 1 hour and 45 minutes long. What time did the tour begin if it ended at 1:35 P.M.?

   _____11:50 A.M._____

4. Tomas took a training class that started at 9:15 A.M. and ended at 12:30 P.M. Between those times, a 45-minute lunch was given. What was the actual length of the training class?

   _____2 hours 30 minutes_____

5. On Sunday, Alexis read from 9:20 A.M. to 10:15 A.M., from 11:35 A.M. to 1:15 P.M., and from 2:30 P.M. to 3:45 P.M. What is a reasonable estimate of the length of time he read on Sunday?

   _____Estimates may vary; a reasonable estimate is 4 hours._____

Find the volume of each prism.

1.

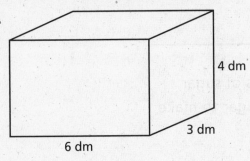

4 dm

3 dm

6 dm

2.

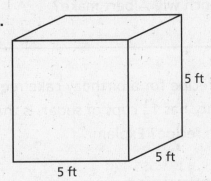

5 ft

5 ft

5 ft

_____72 cu dm_____

_____125 cu ft_____

3.

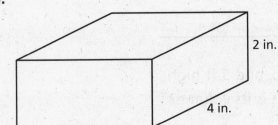

2 in.

4 in.

4 in.

_____32 cu in._____

Solve.

4. a. It takes Mr. Thomas 35 minutes to drive to work. What time should he leave home to arrive at work by 8:45 A.M.?

_____8:10 A.M._____

b. Elena arrived at the library at 11:30 A.M. She left the library at 2:15 P.M. How long was she at the library?

2 hours and 45 minutes

5. The lid of a box is 43 sq cm in area. The volume of the box is 430 cu cm. What is the height of the box?

_10 cm_____

6. Albert is making punch for a party. He combines 1,700 mL of soda with 600 mL of cherry juice. How many liters of punch will Albert make?

2.3 L

7. A recipe for a birthday cake requires $1\frac{1}{8}$ cups of sugar. Mary has $1\frac{1}{3}$ cups of sugar. Is that enough sugar to make the recipe? Explain.

Yes; $\frac{1}{8}$ is less than $\frac{1}{3}$

8. Ralph has 2 kg of carrots and 4 kg of chicken. He plans to use 1.3 kg of carrots and 1,500 g of chicken to make a stew. How many grams of each will not be used?

700 g of carrots and 2,500 g of chicken will not be used.

9. A washing machine is 3 ft wide, 3 ft deep, and 5 ft high. How much floor space will it cover? What is its volume?

It will cover 9 sq ft.; 45 cu ft.

10. **Extended Response** One package weighs 68 ounces. Another package weighs $4\frac{1}{3}$ pounds. Which package is heavier? Explain your answer.

68 ounces is equivalent to 4 pounds 4 ounces. 4 ounces is less than $\frac{1}{3}$ of a pound so the package that weighs $4\frac{1}{3}$ pounds is heavier.

Fill in the circle for the correct answer.

What is the volume of each prism?

1.

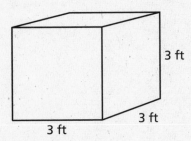

3 ft, 3 ft, 3 ft

Ⓐ 1 cu ft   Ⓑ 9 cu ft

Ⓒ 18 cu ft   Ⓓ 27 cu ft

2.

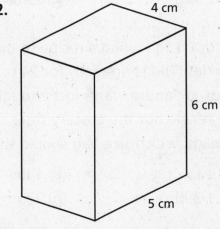

4 cm, 6 cm, 5 cm

Ⓕ 120 cu cm   Ⓖ 115 cu cm

Ⓗ 20 cu cm   Ⓚ 15 cu cm

3.

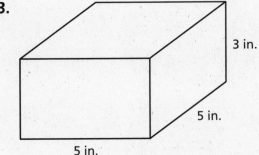

3 in., 5 in., 5 in.

Ⓐ 11 cu in.   Ⓑ 18 cu in.

Ⓒ 60 cu in.   Ⓓ 75 cu in.

4. The area of the bottom of a box is 30 sq cm. The volume of the box is 510 cu cm. What is the height of the box?

Ⓐ 17 cm   Ⓑ 170 cm

Ⓒ 210 cm   Ⓓ 480 cm

Solve.

Show your work.

5. Mark went to sleep at 9:30 P.M. His mother awakened him at 7:15 A.M. How long did Mark sleep?

Ⓕ 8 h   Ⓖ 8 h 45 min

Ⓗ 9 h 15 min   Ⓚ 9 h 45 min

6. Wendy is making a bowl of mixed nuts. She has 1,200 g of peanuts and 900 g of cashews. How many kilograms of nuts will she have?

Show your work.

Ⓕ 1.9 kg   Ⓖ 2.1 kg

Ⓗ 21 kg   Ⓚ 2,100 kg

7. Sandra is following a recipe to make chocolate chip cookies. The recipe calls for 24 ounces of chocolate chips. If Sandra wants just enough chocolate for the recipe but the grocery store only sells 4 sizes of bags, which size bag should she buy?

Ⓐ $\frac{1}{2}$ lb   Ⓑ 1 lb

Ⓒ $1\frac{1}{2}$ lb   Ⓓ 2 lb

8. Quincy is making dinner. He has 4 kg of meat and 4 kg of onions. He plans to use 3.1 kg of meat and 800 g of onions. How many grams of each will not be used?

Ⓕ meat: 100 g   Ⓖ meat: 200 g
  onions: 3,000 g   onions: 600 g

Ⓗ meat: 900 g   Ⓚ meat: 9,000 g
  onions: 3,200 g   onions: 200 g

9. A television is 4 ft wide, 3 ft deep, and 4 ft high. How much floor space will it cover? What is its volume?

Ⓐ 11 sq ft; 11 cu ft   Ⓑ 12 sq ft; 48 cu ft
Ⓒ 19 sq ft; 12 cu ft   Ⓓ 48 sq ft; 19 cu ft

10. A box of books weighs 72 ounces. How many pounds does it weigh?

Ⓕ 4.5   Ⓖ 7.2

Ⓗ 6.3   Ⓚ 16.4

Volume, Capacity, and Weight

What Is Assessed

- Find the volume of a rectangular prism.
- Solve problems involving capacity, mass, and weight.

Explaining the Assessment

1. To introduce the activity tasks, tell students that Gilberto has a planter box and he wants to make a new one with twice the length, width, and height. He thinks doubling the dimensions will give him twice the amount of growing area and that he will need 80 cu dm of soil for the new box. Students will do calculations to show if they agree or disagree with Gilberto.

2. Review the formulas for area and volume.

3. Read the activity aloud with the class.

Possible Responses

Question 1: 4 dm by 10 dm by 8 dm

Question 2: area

Question 3: volume

Question 4: old box: 5 × 4 = 20 sq dm; new box 10 × 8 = 80 sq dm

Question 5: The growing area did not double. It quadrupled. Each dimension was doubled and area involves two dimensions. 2 × 2 = 4, so the area increases by 4 times.

Question 6: old box: 2 × 5 × 4 = 40 cu dm; new box: 4 × 10 × 8 = 320 cu dm

Question 7: No, Gilberto does not have enough soil. He has only 80 cu dm but he needs 320 cu dm.

Question 8: He wants to double each dimension and to find volume you use three dimensions. 2 × 2 × 2 = 8, so the volume increases by 8 times.

ACTIVITY Building a Planter Box

Gilberto has a planter box with the length, width, and height shown.

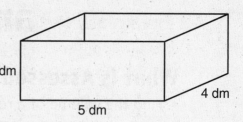

2 dm

5 dm

4 dm

He wants to make a new one. He plans to double the length, width, and height. He has 80 cu dm of soil to put in it. He says the new box will have twice as much growing area and he will have enough soil to fill it. Do you agree or disagree?

1. What will the dimensions of the new planter box be? _____

2. To find the amount of growing area in each box, what do you need to find? Circle the correct measure.

     length   width   height   area   volume

3. To find the amount of soil for each box, what do you need to find? Circle the correct measure.

     length   width   height   area   volume

4. Calculate the growing area of each box. Include units in your answer.

   _____

   _____

5. Did the growing area double? Explain why or why not.

   _____

   _____

6. Calculate the volume of each box.

   _____

   _____

7. Does Gilberto have enough soil? _____

8. Explain why doubling each dimension does not result in twice the volume.

   _____

   _____

Performance Assessment Rubric

An Exemplary Response (4 points)

- Correctly identifies if a problem involves finding length, area, or volume
- Calculates area and volume with no errors and includes the correct units in the final answer
- Correctly observes that doubling dimensions does not result in twice the area or volume
- Uses mathematical language and calculations to efficiently show why doubling dimensions does not double area or volume

A Proficient Response (3 points)

- Correctly identifies if a problem involves finding length, area, or volume
- Calculates area and volume with no errors
- Correctly observes that doubling dimensions does not result in twice the area or volume
- Uses some mathematical language and calculations to show why doubling dimensions does not double area or volume

An Acceptable Response (2 points)

- Correctly identifies if a problem involves finding length, area, or volume
- Calculates area and volume with some calculation errors
- Correctly observes that doubling dimensions does not result in twice the area or volume
- Uses minimal mathematical language and calculations to show why doubling dimensions does not double area or volume

A Limited Response (1 point)

- Correctly identifies if a problem involves finding length, area, or volume
- Attempts to calculate area and volume but makes numerous calculation errors
- May observe that doubling dimensions does not result in twice the area or volume
- Does not explain why doubling dimensions does not result in twice the area or volume

Name _____

Date _____

Solve. Use any method.

1. $\begin{array}{r} 30 \\ \times\ 70 \\ \hline 2{,}100 \end{array}$

2. $\begin{array}{r} 600 \\ \times\ 20 \\ \hline 12{,}000 \end{array}$

3. $\begin{array}{r} 50 \\ \times\ 300 \\ \hline 15{,}000 \end{array}$

4. $\begin{array}{r} 100 \\ \times\ 400 \\ \hline 40{,}000 \end{array}$

5. $\begin{array}{r} 70 \\ \times\ 10 \\ \hline 700 \end{array}$

- -

Name _____

Date _____

Solve. Use mental math when possible.

1. $\begin{array}{r} 100 \\ \times\ 0.46 \\ \hline 46 \end{array}$

2. $\begin{array}{r} 8.4 \\ \times\ 0.01 \\ \hline 0.084 \end{array}$

3. $\begin{array}{r} 3.67 \\ \times\ 10 \\ \hline 36.7 \end{array}$

4. $\begin{array}{r} 0.1 \\ \times\ 5.82 \\ \hline 0.582 \end{array}$

5. $\begin{array}{r} 3.2 \\ \times\ 0.7 \\ \hline 2.24 \end{array}$

Solve. Check your answer.

1. 4)312
   78

2. 6)25,680
   4,280

3. 3)365.4
   121.8

Write the decimal equivalent.

4. $\frac{3}{4} =$ _____ 0.75

5. $\frac{1}{8} =$ _____ 0.125

- -

Solve. Check that your answer is reasonable.

1. 0.1)5.7
   57

2. 0.5)312
   624

3. 0.5)67.8
   135.6

4. Find the median, mode, and mean of this data set:

   31 38 35 33 41 45 44 38 42 39 32

   median: _____ 38

   mode: _____ 38

   mean: _____ 38

Decide whether to multiply or divide. Then solve the problem.

5. Juice glasses need to be filled. Each glass holds 0.2 liters. There
are 4.5 liters of juice. How many glasses can be filled?

_____ divide; 22 glasses _____

_____

Multiply. Use mental math when possible.

1. $20 \times 40 =$ ___800___

2. $300 \times 90 =$ ___27,000___

3. $70 \times 60 =$ ___4,200___

4. $0.005 \times 10 =$ ___0.05___

5. $2 \times 0.7 =$ ___1.4___

6. $0.6 \times 30 =$ ___18___

7. $\begin{array}{r} 45 \\ \times\ 83 \\ \hline 3,735 \end{array}$

8. $\begin{array}{r} 277 \\ \times\ 23 \\ \hline 6,371 \end{array}$

9. $\begin{array}{r} 0.28 \\ \times\ 73 \\ \hline 20.44 \end{array}$

10. $\begin{array}{r} 0.326 \\ \times\ 46 \\ \hline 14.996 \end{array}$

11. Round 0.47 to the nearest tenth. ___0.5___

Round 8.43 to the nearest whole number. ___8___

Round 0.678 to the nearest hundredth. ___0.68___

Solve.

12. Ann can walk 4.2 miles in one hour. How many miles can she walk in 6 hours?

___25.2 miles___

13. Jen earns $10 an hour. If she works 35 hours a week, how much money does she earn in one week?

___$350___

14. Justine's backyard measures 32.5 meters by 26 meters. What is the area of her backyard in square meters?

___845 sq m___

Divide. Check your answer.

15. $6.2 \div 5 =$ ___1.24___

16. $0.54 \div 0.6 =$ ___0.9___

17. $32 \div 0.08 =$ ___400___

Solve. Check that your answer is reasonable.

18. $32\overline{)824}$ _25.75_

19. $63\overline{)3,276}$ _52_

20. $1.6\overline{)115.2}$ _72_

21. $0.38\overline{)988}$ _2,600_

Decide whether to multiply or divide. Then solve the problem.

22. Daniel counted the numbers of cars on the seven levels of the parking garage:
58 61 75 18 65 41 60
What is the mean number of cars on a level of the parking garage?

_____54_____

23. The 18 students in Mrs. Dunn's fifth grade class are having a car wash to raise money for their class trip. They made $873. They will share it equally. How much money will each person get?

divide; $48.50 _____

24. Catherine swam 14.5 laps every day for 22 days. How many laps did she swim in all?

multiply; 319 laps _____

25. Extended Response Explain why when you divide 38.7 by 0.1, the answer is greater than 38.7.

Possible answer: Dividing by 0.1 is the same _____

as multiplying by 10. _____

*Item 25 also assesses the Process Skills of Reasoning and Proof and Connections.

Unit 7 Test, Form A

Fill in the circle for the correct answer.

Multiply. Use mental math when possible.

1. 100
    × 45

    Ⓐ 0.0045   Ⓑ 450
    Ⓒ 4,500   Ⓓ 45,000

2. 6.7
    ×0.01

    Ⓕ 0.0067   Ⓖ 0.067
    Ⓗ 0.67   Ⓚ 67

3. 0.1 × 75 =

    Ⓐ 0.0075   Ⓑ 0.075
    Ⓒ 7.5   Ⓓ 750

4. 10 × 6.34 =

    Ⓕ 0.634   Ⓖ 6.34
    Ⓗ 63.4   Ⓚ 634

5. 35
    × 0.1

    Ⓐ 0.35   Ⓑ 35
    Ⓒ 0.035   Ⓓ 3.5

6. 326
    × 20

    Ⓕ 652   Ⓖ 65,200
    Ⓗ 65.2   Ⓚ 6,520

7. 23
    × 75

    Ⓐ 1,725   Ⓑ 1,735
    Ⓒ 1,825   Ⓓ 2,725

8. 230
    × 567

    Ⓕ 130,310   Ⓖ 130,400
    Ⓗ 130,410   Ⓚ 131,410

9. 0.053
   × 76

    Ⓐ 0.4028   Ⓑ 4.028   Ⓒ 40.28   Ⓓ 402.8

10. $0.007 \times 0.5 =$

  Ⓕ 0.0035   Ⓖ 0.035   Ⓗ 0.35   Ⓚ 3.5

11. Round 0.674 to the nearest hundredth.

  Ⓐ 0.68   Ⓑ 0.7   Ⓒ 0.67   Ⓓ 0.66

12. Bob's truck can travel 22.5 miles on each tank of gasoline. How many miles can it travel on 20 tanks of gasoline?

  Ⓕ 4,500 mi   Ⓖ 4.5 mi   Ⓗ 450 mi   Ⓚ 45 mi

13. Ernie makes 52 cakes every week at the bakery. If there are 52 weeks in a year, how many cakes will he make in one year?

  Ⓐ 104 cakes   Ⓑ 2,704 cakes   Ⓒ 52 cakes   Ⓓ 1,614 cakes

14. Gail's pool measures 22.2 feet by 30 feet. What is the area of Gail's pool in square feet?

  Ⓕ 666 sq ft   Ⓖ 104.4 sq ft   Ⓗ 52.2 sq ft   Ⓚ 492.84 sq ft

     Unit 7 Test, Form B

Divide. Check that your answer is reasonable.

15. $8.6 \div 4$

Ⓐ 0.215   Ⓑ 2.15   Ⓒ 21.5   Ⓓ 20.15

16. $0.8 \div 0.2$

Ⓕ 0.4   Ⓖ 0.04   Ⓗ 4   Ⓚ 16

17. $26 \div 0.13$

Ⓐ 0.200   Ⓑ 20   Ⓒ 200   Ⓓ 0.002

18. $342 \div 30$

Ⓕ 0.114   Ⓖ 1.14   Ⓗ 114   Ⓚ 11.4

19. $63\overline{)2,646}$

Ⓐ 402   Ⓑ 420   Ⓒ 42   Ⓓ 4.2

20. $2.6\overline{)96.2}$

Ⓕ 38   Ⓖ 37   Ⓗ 39   Ⓚ 41

21. $0.82\overline{)1,312}$

Ⓐ 1,600   Ⓑ 160   Ⓒ 0.160   Ⓓ 0.0016

Choose the correct operation and solution to the problem.

22. Aquariums at a pet shop have the following numbers of fish:

    12 43 15 19 11 4 22

    Which is the mean number of fish in an aquarium?

    Ⓕ add and multiply; 15   Ⓖ subtract and multiply; 17
    Ⓗ add and divide; 18   Ⓚ add and subtract; 20

23. The 14 members of the Johnsonville Swim Team sold raffle tickets to raise money for a trip to Florida. They made $644, and they will share it equally. How much money will each person get?

    Ⓐ divide; $46   Ⓑ add; $658
    Ⓒ multiply; $9,016   Ⓓ divide; $0.644

24. Anthony drives 26.3 miles to and from work, 5 days a week. How many miles does Anthony drive in 2 weeks?

    Ⓕ multiply; 131.5 miles   Ⓖ multiply; 263 miles
    Ⓗ divide; 2.63 miles   Ⓚ divide; 5.26 miles

Which explanation best answers the question?

25. When you divide 84.6 by 0.1, why is the answer greater than 84.6?

    Ⓐ Dividing by 0.1 is the same as multiplying by 10.
    Ⓑ Dividing by 0.1 is the same as multiplying by 100.
    Ⓒ When you divide, the quotient is always bigger than the dividend.
    Ⓓ Dividing is the same as multiplying.

    *Item 25 also assesses the Process Skills of Reasoning and Proof and Connections.

Multiplication and Division with Whole Numbers and Decimals

What Is Assessed

- Multiply and divide whole numbers using multiples of ten.
- Convert measurements into the same unit.
- Analyze data.
- Explain procedures and results.

Explaining the Assessment

1. Set the context for the task by telling students that animals can run at very different speeds. A speed always involves two units of measurement – distance and time. It tells you how far an animal can travel in a given amount of time.

2. Read the task aloud with the class.

Possible Responses

Question 1: The chicken runs 1,520 feet in 2 minutes. The squirrel runs 1,000 feet in 1 minute, so it can run $2 \times 1,000$ ft = 2,000 feet in 2 minutes. The squirrel is faster so it will get to the other side first.

Question 2:

Chicken: 1,520 ft ÷ 2 = 760 ft

Squirrel: 1,000 ft

Antelope: 60 miles in one hour ÷ 60 minutes = 1 mile in one minute

1 mile in one minute = 5,280 ft in one minute

Question 3:

The chicken travels 760 ft in one minute. The antelope travels 5,280 ft in one minute. 5,280 is about 7 times 760.

Some students may round numbers to 1,000 and estimate 5 times faster.

Some may round to 800 and 5,000 and estimate 6 times faster.

Some may use $7 \times 8 = 56$ and estimate 8 times faster.

ACTIVITY Running Times

A chicken can run 1,520 feet in 2 minutes.

If an antelope always ran at its top speed, it could run 60 miles in one hour.

1. A squirrel can run 1,000 feet in 1 minute. If the chicken and the squirrel run across a road, which animal will be first to get to the other side? Explain.

2. How many feet can each animal run in one minute? Show your work.

    Chicken _____

    Squirrel _____

    Antelope _____

3. Estimate how many times faster an antelope is than a chicken. Check your estimate by multiplying.

Math Expressions

A79

Unit 7 Performance Assessment

Performance Assessment Rubric

An Exemplary Response (4 points)

- Always includes correct units of measurement
- Correctly converts speeds so that all show number of feet in one minute
- Checks and refines estimates until the best whole-number estimate is found

A Proficient Response (3 points)

- Always includes correct units of measurement
- Converts speeds correctly and compares them correctly
- Finds a reasonable estimate by rounding numbers and checking

An Acceptable Response (2 points)

- Shows all measurements and computations used to make comparisons; includes most units of measurement
- Compares at least 2 of the speeds correctly
- Makes a reasonable estimate, but doesn't show checking of results

A Limited Response (1 point)

- Some units may be converted incorrectly, or not included
- Some computations and comparisons may be incorrect
- Estimates may be unrealistic

Fill in the circle for the correct answer.

1. Which is a simplified form of the expression $4^3 \times 12$?

   Ⓐ 768

   Ⓑ 192

   Ⓒ 48

   Ⓓ 16

2. Which shows the simplified form of the expression
   $(3 + 7) \div 5 + 7 \times 3$?

   Ⓕ 2

   Ⓖ 18

   Ⓗ 23

   Ⓚ 24.563

3. Which is the simplified form of $\sqrt{25}$?

   Ⓐ 7

   Ⓑ 6

   Ⓒ 6.5

   Ⓓ 5

4. Which is the simplified form of $\sqrt{100}$?

   Ⓕ 50

   Ⓖ 4×25

   Ⓗ 10

   Ⓚ 10^2

5. Which is the value of n for the equation $3^n = 81$?

   Ⓐ $n = 3$

   Ⓑ $n = 4$

   Ⓒ $n = 5$

   Ⓓ $n = 9$

6. Which shows the prime factorization of 88?

   Ⓕ $2 \times 2 \times 11$

   Ⓖ 8×11

   Ⓗ $4 \times 4 \times 11$

   Ⓚ $2 \times 2 \times 2 \times 11$

Math Expressions

A85

Unit 8 Test, Form B

7. It takes Ron 17 minutes to change a tire at the garage. Which equation and solution would correctly answer the question, "How many tires could Ron change in 221 minutes?"

Ⓐ $221 \div 17 = t; t = 15$

Ⓑ $221 \times 17 = t; t = 3{,}757$

Ⓒ $221 \div t = 17; t = 15$

Ⓓ $221 \div t = 17; t = 13$

8. Which values of the variable make the inequality true?
$v + 17 > 52$

Ⓕ 36, 37, 38

Ⓖ 34, 35, 36

Ⓗ 35, 36, 37

Ⓚ 33, 35, 37

9. Which is the correct equation for this function table?

Equation: ?						
Input (x)	5	10	12	17	42	74
Output (y)	7	17	21	31	81	145

Ⓐ $y = 2x - 3$

Ⓑ $x = 2y + 3$

Ⓒ $y = 2x + 3$

Ⓓ $x = 2y - 3$

10. Which graph could be used to solve the problem?

Brianna charges $5 for a babysitting job, plus $3 for each hour of babysitting. How much will she earn for babysitting the Carr's children for 3 hours?

Ⓕ
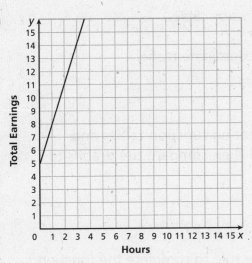

Ⓖ
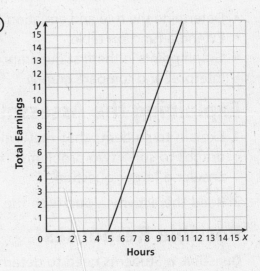

Ⓗ
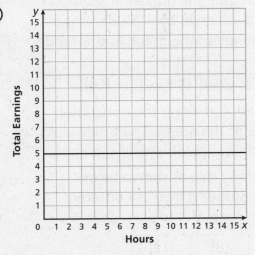

Ⓚ
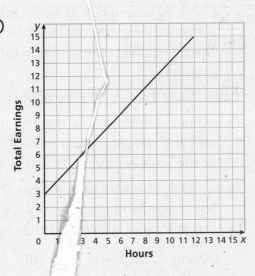

Algebra, Functions, and Graphs

What Is Assessed

- Determine the rule and equation for a function table.
- Extend a function table.
- Graph points in the first quadrant of the coordinate plane.
- Interpret and compare graphs.

Explaining the Assessment

1. Explain to students that they will be creating function tables and graphs to solve two problems. They will then compare the graphs to answer a larger question.

2. Read the activity aloud with the class.

Possible Responses

Question 1: Students need to determine the rule to complete the function table. Since there are 2 ounces of shampoo used to 3 heads of hair, one way to describe the rule is that each time the ounces of shampoo increases by 2, the heads of hair washed increases by 3. Students use the points from the function table to complete the graph and extend the line.

Question 2: It takes 10 ounces of shampoo to wash 15 heads of hair.

Question 3: Students find the line for 15 washings along the horizontal axis and follow that up to meet the line of the graph. Then they look at the scale on the vertical axis to determine the ounces of shampoo.

Question 4: Students should label the function table as shown below. Some possible number pairs are shown. Students may use different number pairs. Make sure they are in the ratio of 4 to 5.

Shampoo (ounces)	[0]	[4]	[8]	[12]
Heads of Hair Washed	[0]	[5]	[10]	[15]

Question 5: Students should label the graph as in Question 1: They should enter the ordered pairs from the function table and draw the line through the points.

Question 6: It takes 12 ounces of shampoo to wash 15 customers' hair.

Question 7: Students compare the results of the graphs. Since it takes more shampoo to wash the hair of the same number of customers, the new shampoo is less economical than the old shampoo.

Name _____ Date _____

ACTIVITY Sara's Hair Salon

Sara owns a hair styling salon. She uses a special shampoo. She can wash the hair of 3 customers with only 2 oz of shampoo.

1. Complete the function table and graph the points to find how many ounces of shampoo Sara needs to wash 15 customers' hair.

Shampoo (ounces)	0	2	4	6
Heads of Hair Washed	0	3	6	9

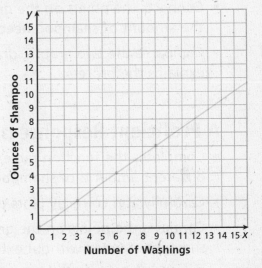

2. How many ounces of shampoo are needed to wash 15 customers' hair?

_____

3. How did you determine the answer to the problem?

_____

The shampoo company changed their formula. It now takes 4 ounces of shampoo to wash 5 heads of hair.

4. Prepare a function table that reflects the new information about the shampoo.

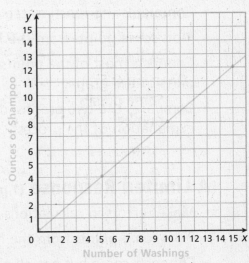

5. Label the graph. Graph the points from the function table. Determine how many ounces of shampoo are needed to wash 15 heads of hair using the new formula.

6. How many ounces of shampoo are needed to wash 15 customers' hair?

_____

7. Is the new shampoo more economical or less economical to use than the old formula? Explain how you determined your answer.

_____

Performance Assessment Rubric

An Exemplary Response (4 points)

- Completes the function tables with correct calculations for the different amounts of shampoo.
- Carefully and correctly plots the points from the function tables.
- Connects the points on the graphs and extends the lines to determine the amount of shampoo needed.
- Compares the two graphs, draws an accurate conclusion, and clearly explains the process.

A Proficient Response (3 points)

- Completes the function tables with correct calculations for the different amounts of shampoo.
- Carefully and correctly plots the points from the function tables.
- Connects the points on the graphs and determines the amount of shampoo needed without extending the line.
- Compares the two graphs, draws a conclusion, and explains the process.

An Acceptable Response (2 points)

- Completes the function tables but may make errors in calculations.
- Plots some points from the function tables.
- Connects most of the points on the graphs, but may mislabel some parts of the graph.
- Compares the two graphs, draws a conclusion, and gives a minimal explanation of the process.

A Limited Response (1 point)

- Makes errors in calculations when completing the function tables.
- Plots some points from the function tables.
- Connects some but not all of the points on the graphs; omits labels.
- Makes an error in comparing the information from the graphs, and gives little or no explanation.

Solve. Simplify your answers.

1. $8 \times \frac{1}{2} =$ _____ 4 _____

2. $\frac{1}{8} \times 160 =$ _____ 20 _____

3. $\frac{5}{6} \times 9 =$ $\frac{45}{6} = \frac{15}{2}$

4. $\frac{3}{4} \times \frac{7}{12} =$ $\frac{21}{48} = \frac{7}{16}$

5. $1\frac{1}{4} \times 1\frac{1}{5} =$ $\frac{30}{20} = \frac{3}{2} = 1\frac{1}{2}$

- -

Unit 9
Quick Quiz 2

Name

Date

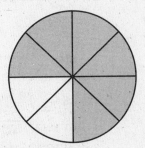

1. Write the fraction and decimal equivalent for the shaded part of the circle.

Fraction: $\frac{6}{8} = \frac{3}{4}$

Decimal: _____ 0.75 _____

2. Give the fraction equivalent in simplest form.

$0.35 =$ $\frac{35}{100} = \frac{7}{20}$

Solve. Simplify your answers.

3. $15 \div \frac{1}{3} =$ _____ 45 _____

4. $\frac{1}{3} \div 8 =$ $\frac{1}{24}$

5. How is adding fractions different from multiplying them?

Answers will vary. _____

_____

_____

1. Rewrite $28 \times \frac{1}{4}$ as a division expression and solve.

   $\underline{\quad 28 \div 4 = 7 \quad}$

2. Rewrite $\frac{7}{8} \div \frac{1}{3}$ as a multiplication expression and solve.

   $\underline{\frac{7}{8} \times 3 = \frac{21}{8} = 2\frac{5}{8}\quad}$

Solve. Show your work.

3. $20 \div \frac{1}{5} = \underline{\quad 10.0 \quad}$

4. $\frac{12}{3} \div \frac{6}{16} = \underline{\quad \frac{32}{3} = 10\frac{2}{3} \quad}$

5. Find the mean of this data set:

   $\frac{1}{3} \quad \frac{5}{12} \quad \frac{1}{2} \quad \frac{5}{8} \quad \frac{2}{3} \quad \frac{3}{8} \quad \frac{3}{4}$

   $\underline{\quad \frac{11}{21} \quad}$

Solve. Show your work.

1. $\frac{1}{8} \times 3 =$ _____ $\frac{3}{8}$

2. $\frac{4}{6} \times 3 =$ _____ $\frac{12}{6} = 2$

3. $\frac{1}{7} \times 21 =$ _____ $\frac{21}{7} = 3$

4. $\frac{2}{4} \times 40 =$ _____ $\frac{80}{4} = 20$

5. $\frac{5}{6} \times \frac{3}{4} =$ _____ $\frac{15}{24} = \frac{5}{8}$

6. $\frac{3}{5} \times \frac{6}{9} =$ _____ $\frac{18}{45} = \frac{2}{5}$

7. Jason worked at the grocery store for $\frac{5}{6}$ of an hour. He spent $\frac{2}{3}$ of that time stocking shelves. For how long did he stock shelves?

_____ $\frac{10}{18} = \frac{5}{9}$ of an hour _____

Give the decimal equivalent.

8. $\frac{1}{5} =$ _____ 0.2

9. $\frac{1}{2} =$ _____ 0.5

Give the fraction equivalent.

10. $0.125 =$ _____ $\frac{1}{8}$

11. $0.75 =$ _____ $\frac{3}{4}$

12. How is adding fractions different from multiplying and dividing them?

_____ Answers will vary. _____

_____

_____

Solve. Show your work.

13. $4 \div 6 =$ _____ $0.\overline{6}$

14. $4 \div \frac{1}{6} =$ _____ 24

15. $4 \div \frac{2}{6} =$ _____ 12

16. $\frac{4}{5} \div \frac{3}{4} =$ _____ $\frac{16}{15} = 1\frac{1}{15}$

17. $\frac{3}{8} \div \frac{2}{3} =$ _____ $\frac{9}{16}$

18. $\frac{1}{5} \div 6 =$ _____ $\frac{1}{30}$

19. Find the mean of this set of data:

$\frac{1}{4}$ $\frac{1}{8}$ $\frac{7}{8}$ $\frac{5}{8}$ $\frac{1}{2}$ $\frac{3}{4}$ $\frac{3}{8}$

_____ $\frac{1}{2}$ _____

20. **Extended Response** Will $5 \div \frac{3}{4}$ be more or less than 5? Explain why.

More, because dividing by $\frac{3}{4}$ is the same as multiplying by $1\frac{1}{3}$.

_____

_____

_____

_____

*Item 20 also assesses the Process Skills of Connections and Reasoning and Proof.

Fill in the circle for the correct answer.

Solve.

1. $\frac{5}{6} \times 15 =$

   Ⓐ $\frac{5}{21}$ Ⓑ $\frac{75}{90}$

   Ⓒ $\frac{20}{6}$ Ⓓ $\frac{25}{2}$

2. $\frac{4}{7} \times \frac{3}{8} =$

   Ⓕ $\frac{3}{14}$ Ⓖ $\frac{7}{15}$

   Ⓗ $\frac{12}{8}$ Ⓚ $\frac{12}{7}$

3. $\frac{1}{4} \times 16 =$

   Ⓐ 64   Ⓑ 4

   Ⓒ 8   Ⓓ 12

4. $\frac{2}{5} \times 50 =$

   Ⓕ 20   Ⓖ 10

   Ⓗ 25   Ⓚ 5

5. $\frac{7}{8} \times \frac{3}{4} =$

   Ⓐ $\frac{24}{28}$ Ⓑ $\frac{10}{12}$

   Ⓒ $\frac{21}{32}$ Ⓓ $\frac{21}{12}$

6. $\frac{2}{3} \times 30 =$

   Ⓕ 20   Ⓖ 25

   Ⓗ 10   Ⓚ 60

7. Bert swam in the pool for $\frac{7}{8}$ of an hour. He spent $\frac{1}{6}$ of that time treading water. For how long did Bert tread water?

   Ⓐ $\frac{8}{14}$ hour   Ⓑ $\frac{7}{48}$ hour   Ⓒ $\frac{42}{8}$ hours   Ⓓ $\frac{6}{2}$ hours

What is the decimal equivalent?

8. $\frac{1}{4}$

   Ⓕ 0.25   Ⓖ 0.75

   Ⓗ 0.4   Ⓚ 4.0

9. $\frac{2}{3}$

   Ⓐ 0.23   Ⓑ $0.\overline{3}$

   Ⓒ 0.03   Ⓓ $0.\overline{6}$

What is the fraction equivalent?

10. 0.75

   Ⓕ $\frac{75}{10}$ Ⓖ $\frac{1}{4}$

   Ⓗ $\frac{3}{4}$ Ⓚ $\frac{2}{3}$

11. 0.125

   Ⓐ $\frac{2}{8}$ Ⓑ $\frac{1}{8}$

   Ⓒ $\frac{1}{4}$ Ⓓ $\frac{3}{4}$

12. Which has a value less than $\frac{3}{4}$?

 Ⓕ $\frac{3}{4} + \frac{1}{2}$ Ⓖ $\frac{1}{2} + \frac{3}{4}$ Ⓗ $\frac{1}{2} \times \frac{3}{4}$ Ⓚ $2 \times \frac{3}{4}$

Solve.

13. $2 \div 3 =$

 Ⓐ $0.\overline{6}$ Ⓑ 0.23

 Ⓒ $0.\overline{3}$ Ⓓ 1.5

14. $2 \div \frac{1}{3} =$

 Ⓕ 1.5 Ⓖ 6

 Ⓗ 1 Ⓚ $\frac{3}{2}$

15. $2 \div \frac{2}{3} =$

 Ⓐ $\frac{4}{3}$ Ⓑ 1

 Ⓒ 3 Ⓓ 9

16. $\frac{5}{6} \div \frac{3}{7} =$

 Ⓕ $\frac{35}{18}$ Ⓖ $\frac{8}{13}$

 Ⓗ $\frac{15}{42}$ Ⓚ $\frac{18}{35}$

17. $\frac{6}{8} \div \frac{1}{4} =$

 Ⓐ $\frac{6}{32}$ Ⓑ $\frac{7}{12}$

 Ⓒ 4 Ⓓ 3

18. $\frac{1}{4} \div 9 =$

 Ⓕ 36 Ⓖ $\frac{3}{6}$

 Ⓗ $\frac{1}{36}$ Ⓚ $\frac{9}{4}$

19. Which is the mean of this set of data?

 $\frac{1}{5}$ $\frac{3}{8}$ $\frac{13}{20}$ $\frac{5}{8}$ $\frac{3}{5}$ $\frac{9}{20}$ $\frac{3}{10}$

 Ⓐ $\frac{8}{40}$ Ⓑ $\frac{16}{35}$ Ⓒ $\frac{16}{5}$ Ⓓ $\frac{5}{7}$

20. Will $5 \div \frac{3}{4}$ be more or less than 5? How much more or less?

 Ⓕ more; $1\frac{2}{3}$ Ⓖ less; $1\frac{2}{3}$ Ⓗ more; $4\frac{1}{4}$ Ⓚ less; $4\frac{1}{4}$

*Item 20 also assesses the Process Skills of Connections and Reasoning and Proof.

Multiplication and Division with Fractions

What Is Assessed

- Multiply fractions and mixed numbers.
- Relate fractional operations.
- Divide fractions and mixed numbers.

Explaining the Assessment

1. Tell students that they will be making multiplication and division equations with fractions. First they will finish partially completed equations.

2. Read the activity aloud with the class.

3. After completing Question 1, ask students if they can simplify the answer.

4. Prompt them to use logic and a Guess and Check strategy to find the missing numbers in exercise 3. For a product of $\frac{2}{5}$, the denominator of one factor has to be 5.

Possible Responses

Question 1: The product $\frac{9}{24}$ simplifies to $\frac{3}{8}$. Some students may write the simplified product as the initial answer and not need to simplify further.

Question 2: $\frac{3}{5} \times \frac{4}{6} = \frac{2}{5}$. The numerators and denominators can be in any order.

Question 3: Either fractional factor of the product can be used for the divisor in the division equation.

Question 4: Students should mention that multiplying by a fraction gives the same answer as dividing by the inverse of the fraction.

ACTIVITY Fraction Puzzles

1. Complete the fraction multiplication. Simplify the answer if possible.

Simplified answer:

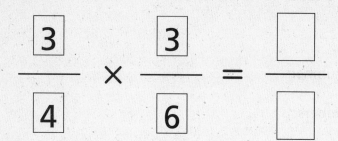

$$\frac{\boxed{3}}{\boxed{4}} \times \frac{\boxed{3}}{\boxed{6}} = \frac{\boxed{}}{\boxed{}}$$

2. Use the numbers 3, 4, 5, and 6 to make a multiplication with a product of $\frac{2}{5}$.

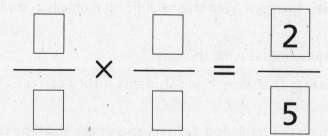

$$\frac{\boxed{}}{\boxed{}} \times \frac{\boxed{}}{\boxed{}} = \frac{\boxed{2}}{\boxed{5}}$$

3. Create your own multiplication sentence using any numbers. Then change it to an equivalent division sentence. Simplify the answer if possible.

Simplified answers:

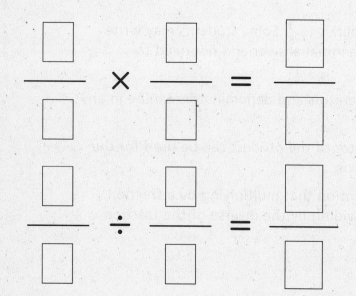

$$\frac{\boxed{}}{\boxed{}} \times \frac{\boxed{}}{\boxed{}} = \frac{\boxed{}}{\boxed{}}$$

$$\frac{\boxed{}}{\boxed{}} \div \frac{\boxed{}}{\boxed{}} = \frac{\boxed{}}{\boxed{}}$$

4. How do you know your multiplication and division sentences above are equivalent?

_____

_____

Performance Assessment Rubric

An Exemplary Response (4 points)

- Includes all the numbers to complete each equation correctly
- Simplifies fractions correctly
- Writes the related division equation correctly and explains thoroughly, using mathematical language, why the multiplication and division sentences are equivalent

A Proficient Response (3 points)

- Includes most of the numbers to complete each equation correctly
- Simplifies fractions correctly
- Writes the related division equation correctly, and explains why the multiplication and division sentences are equivalent

An Acceptable Response (2 points)

- Includes many of the numbers to complete each equation correctly
- May not simplify all fractions that are not in simplest form
- Writes the related division equation correctly, but may not explain why the multiplication and division sentences are equivalent

A Limited Response (1 point)

- Makes many errors in each equation
- Does not simplify fractions correctly
- Writes incorrect factors in related division equation

1. Show two ways to extend the pattern. Draw the next four terms.

2. Write an equation to represent the function. Then complete the table.

r	1	2	3	4	5
t	1	3	5	7	9

$t = 2r - 1$

3. Name the transformation used to create each figure.

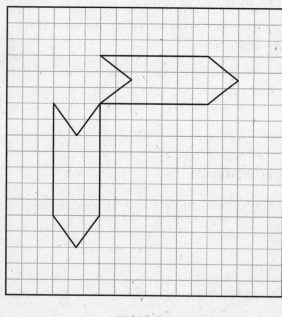

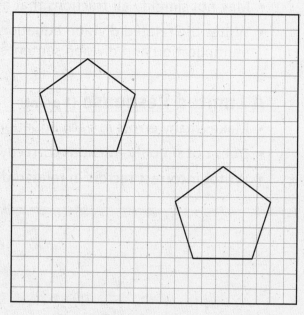

rotation   translation

4. Reflect the triangle across the given line.

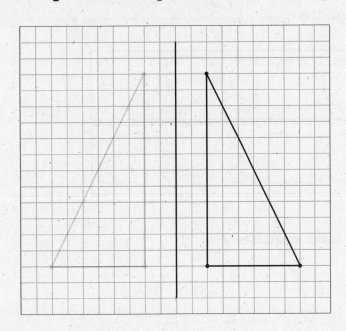

5. Translate each point of the trapezoid down 3 units on the coordinate grid. What are the vertices of the translated trapezoid?

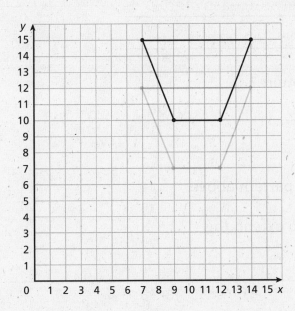

____(7,12)____   ____(9,7)____   ____(12,7)____   ____(14,12)____

1. Show two different ways to extend the pattern. Draw the next three terms for each pattern.

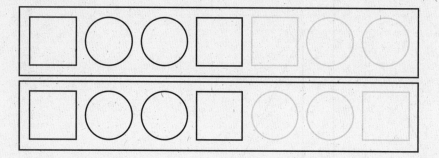

Use the pattern below to solve exercises 2–4.

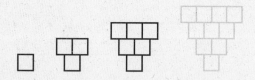

2. What type of pattern is this? How do you know?

It is a growing pattern because each step

has more squares than the step before.

3. What is the rule for this pattern?

Add a row on top that has one more square

than the row below.

4. Draw the next term of the pattern above.

5. Show two different ways to extend this numerical pattern.

$\frac{1}{2}, \frac{1}{2}, \frac{1}{4}$	$\frac{1}{2}, \frac{1}{2}, \frac{1}{4}, \frac{1}{2}, \frac{1}{2}, \frac{1}{4}$
$\frac{1}{2}, \frac{1}{2}, \frac{1}{4}$	$\frac{1}{4}, \frac{1}{2}, \frac{1}{2}, \frac{1}{4}, \frac{1}{4}, \frac{1}{2}$

6. Write an equation to represent the function. Then complete the table.

a	1	2	3	4	5
b	6	10	14	18	22

$b = 4a + 2$

7. Describe the transformation that resulted in triangle $A'B'C'$.

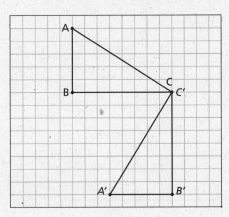

It is a 90° rotation around point C.

8. What do you know about the numerical relationship between the coordinates for triangle ABC and the coordinates for triangle $A'B'C'$?

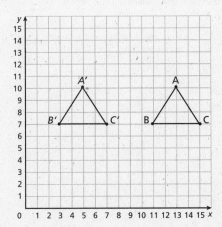

The x-coordinates for $A'B'C'$ are each 8 less than the coordinates for ABC.

The y-coordinates are the same for both triangles.

Unit 10 Test, Form A

9. Rotate the triangle 270° clockwise around point B. Where are the vertices of the rotated triangle?

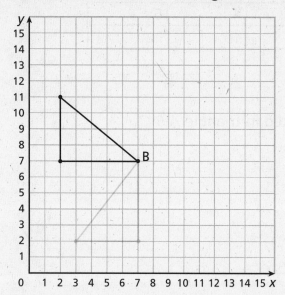

(3, 2), (7, 2), (7,7)

10. Extended Response Plot the points (1, 6) and (14, 6) and use your ruler to draw a line through the points. Draw a triangle with vertices (2, 7), (2, 11), and (7, 7). Reflect the triangle over the line you drew and record the vertices.

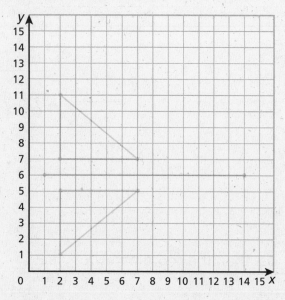

Reflected triangle: (2, 1), (2, 5), (7, 5).

Unit 10 Test, Form A

Fill in the circle for the correct answer.

1. Which shows the next three terms in the pattern?

(A)    (B)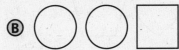

(C) 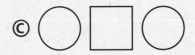   (D)

2. Which arrangement shows a growing pattern?

(F)

(G)

(H)

(J)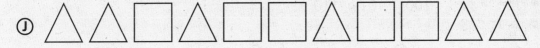

3. Which arrangement shows a shrinking pattern?

(A)

(B)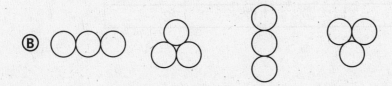

(C)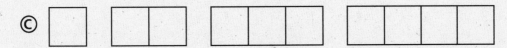

(D)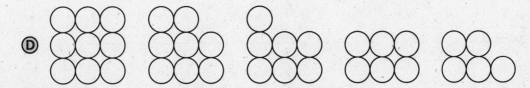

4. Which shows the next three terms in the pattern?

Ⓕ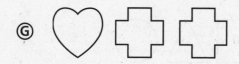

Ⓖ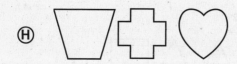

Ⓗ

Ⓚ

5. Which is the next term in the numerical pattern?

   1   10   11   100   101   110

Ⓐ 1000   Ⓑ 111   Ⓒ 1001   Ⓓ 1100

6. Which equation represents the function shown in the table?

x	1	2	3	4	5
y	2	7	12	17	22

Ⓕ $x = 5y - 3$

Ⓖ $x = 5y + 3$

Ⓗ $y = 5x - 3$

Ⓚ $y = 5x + 3$

7. Which best describes the transformation shown?

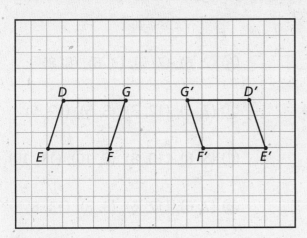

Ⓐ turn

Ⓑ translation

Ⓒ rotation

Ⓓ reflection

8. Which best describes the mathematical relationship between the coordinates of triangle *WXY* and its translation *W'X'Y'*?

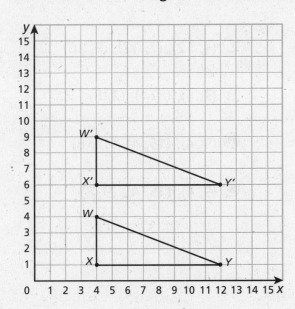

Ⓕ The *x*-coordinates are the same, but the *y*-coordinates are 5 less.

Ⓖ The *x*-coordinates are the same, but the *y*-coordinates are 5 greater.

Ⓗ The *x*-coordinates are 5 greater, and the *y*-coordinates are 5 greater.

Ⓚ The *x*-coordinates are 5 greater, and the *y*-coordinates are the same.

Unit 10 Test, Form B

9. Parallelogram *GHJK* is translated up 3 units and right 5 units.
   Which are the coordinates of *G'H'J'K'*?

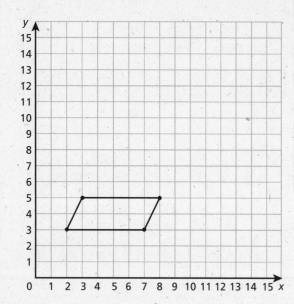

Ⓐ (2, 6), (7, 5), (3, 8), (8, 8)

Ⓑ (7, 3), (12, 3), (8, 5), (12, 5)

Ⓒ (5, 8), (10, 8), (6, 10), (11, 10)

Ⓓ (7, 6), (12, 6), (8, 8), (13, 8)

10. Triangle *RST* is reflected across the line shown. Which are the
    coordinates of *R'S'T'*?

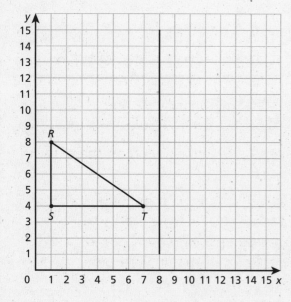

Ⓕ (1, 12), (7, 12), (9, 16)

Ⓖ (2, 4), (8, 4), (2, 8)

Ⓗ (9, 4), (15, 4), (15, 8)

Ⓚ (9, 4), (15, 4), (9, 8)

Patterns and Transformations

What Is Assessed

- Recognize and complete rotations, reflections, and translations.
- Read points on a coordinate grid.
- Identify patterns in motion geometry.

Explaining the Assessment

1. Tell students that they will be making transformations of a triangle on a coordinate grid and finding out how the transformations change the coordinates.

2. Read the activity aloud with the class.

3. After completing Question 1, have students cut out the triangle. As an option, they may glue the triangle on cardboard and use it to trace transformed triangles on the blank grid. If colored pencils are available, you may wish to have students use one color to show the flip, a different color to show the rotation, and a third color to show the translations.

Possible Responses

Question 1: The coordinates are (1, 6), (1, 3), and (5, 3).

Question 2: The triangle may be flipped either horizontally or vertically and repositioned on the grid so that vertices are on grid points.

Question 3: The triangle may be rotated any multiple of 90° and repositioned on the grid so that vertices are on grid points.

Question 4: The triangle may be translated and repositioned on the grid so that vertices are on grid points.

Question 5: Every x-coordinate will increase by 1 if the triangle is translated 1 to the right, or decrease by 1 if it is translated 1 to the left. Every y-coordinate will decrease by the amount of the downward slide or increase by the amount of the upward slide.

ACTIVITY Triangle Transformations

1. Write the coordinates of the vertices of the triangle.

   _____

   _____

   _____

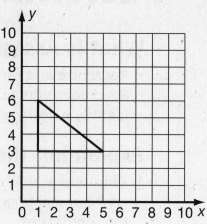

Cut out the triangle.

2. Flip the triangle and place it on the blank grid with its vertices on the grid. Write the new coordinates of its vertices here.

   _____   _____   _____

3. Rotate the triangle and place it on the blank grid with its vertices on the grid. Write the new coordinates of its vertices.

   _____

   _____

   _____

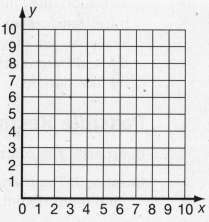

4. Translate the triangle to two different new positions on the grid. Write the new coordinates of the vertices for each.

   _____   _____

   _____   _____

   _____   _____

5. For each translated triangle, describe the pattern that changes the original coordinates to the new coordinates.

   _____

   _____

Unit 10 Performance Assessment

Performance Assessment Rubric

An Exemplary Response (4 points)

- Writes all the coordinates correctly
- Performs each transformation correctly
- Explains the translation patterns logically

A Proficient Response (3 points)

- Writes all original coordinates correctly
- Lists correct coordinates for most of the transformed vertices
- States correct rules for the translation patterns

An Acceptable Response (2 points)

- Writes all original coordinates correctly
- Makes several errors in transformed coordinates
- Describes the pattern for just one of the translated triangles

A Limited Response (1 point)

- Some original coordinates may be stated incorrectly
- Makes many errors in transformed coordinates
- Does not recognize a pattern in the translated coordinates

1. Circle the Multiplication Column Table. Explain why the other table is not a Multiplication Column Table.

0	0
1	6
2	12
3	18
4	24
5	30

0	0
1	6
2	12
3	19
4	26
5	33

The second column in the second table doesn't increase at an even rate.

The first two numbers increase by 6, then they increase by 7.

Which of these are Multiplication Column Situations? For each one that is:
- tell the unit and the group per unit.
- write the situation using the word *per*.

2. There are 9 plants in every row of a corn field. The field has 7 rows.

Multiplication Column Situation. Unit: row, Group: 9 plants. The corn field has 9 plants per row.

3. Katie walks 2 miles every school day and 5 miles each weekend.

This is not a Multiplication Column Situation.

4. Alton sends 3 postcards every time he goes on vacation.

Multiplication Column Situation. Unit: vacation, Group: 3 postcards. Alton sends 3 postcards per vacation.

5. Make a Ratio Table for
this situation. Be sure to
label your table.

A garden design calls for
7 bushes for every 5 trees.

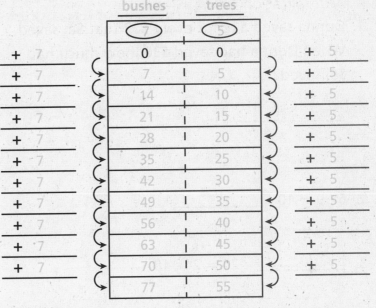

Ratio Table

bushes	trees
7	5
0	0
7	5
14	10
21	15
28	20
35	25
42	30
49	35
56	40
63	45
70	50
77	55

Complete the Factor Puzzle and solve the problem.

1. Donna saved $12 for every $22 that Sal saved. When Donna had saved $30, how much had Sal saved?

   _____ $55 _____

	6	11	
2	12	22	2
5	30	55	5
	6	11	

2. 6 : 9 = 10 : _____ 15 _____

   Show your work.

3. _____ 32 _____ : 24 = 24 : 18

4. Andy is looking for frogs and turtles in the lake. For every 4 frogs he has seen, he has also seen 10 turtles. If he has seen 60 turtles, how many frogs has he seen?

   24 frogs _____

5. A painter makes pink paint by mixing 4 cans of white paint with 7 cans of red paint. If the painter uses 35 cans of red paint, how many cans of white paint should she use to make the pink paint?

   20 cans of white paint _____

Name _____ Date _____

● **Complete each sentence.**

1. _____ 50 _____ is 25% of 200.

2. 6 is _____ 15 _____ % of 40.

3. 16 is 5% of _____ 320 _____ .

Solve each problem.   *Show your work.*

4. Heather had $45 when she went to the zoo. She
   spent 40% of her money. How much did she have left
   when she came home?

   $27 _____

● 5. A bag of 25 marbles contains 13 green marbles. If one
   marble is picked from the bag, what is the probability
   that it is green? Express your answer as a percent.

   52% _____

●

Is each pair of figures similar? Circle *yes* or *no*.

1.

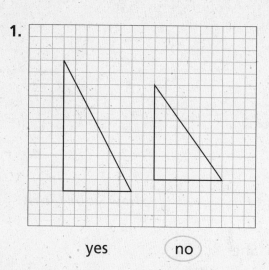

yes   (no)

2. Draw a similar rectangle with sides twice as long as the given rectangle.

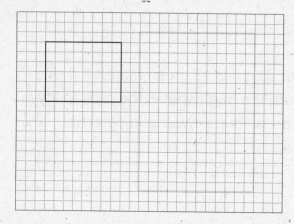

3. Write the missing measurement.

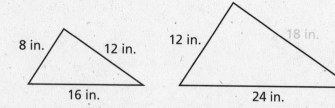

8 in.   12 in.   16 in.

12 in.   18 in.   24 in.

Use the scale to solve for *n*. Show your work.

4. 2 in. = 56 mi

5 in. = *n* mi

n = 140 mi

5. A map has a scale of 1 cm = 8 km. The actual distance from Pittsburgh to Cleveland is 181 km. What length would show that distance on the map?

$22\frac{5}{8}$ cm
_____

6. This scale drawing shows the distance from Greensburg to Johnstown is 32 miles. What is the distance from Greensburg to Monroeville?

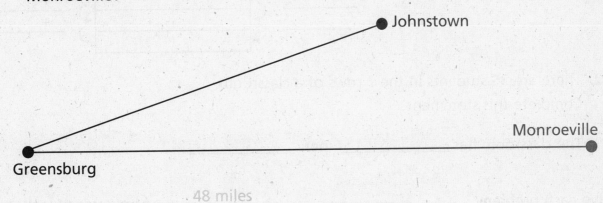

48 miles
_____

7. Use the scale drawing to find the actual measurements.

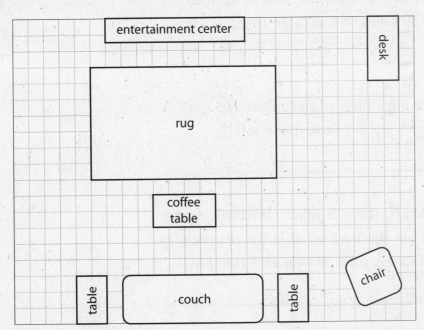

Length of couch: ___9 feet___   Scale: — = 1 ft

Area of rug: ___7 × 12 = 84 square feet___

1. Make a Ratio Table for this situation. Be sure to label your table.

   A bead design calls for 8 red beads for every 3 green beads.

Ratio Table

	red		green	
	(8)		(3)	
+ 8	0		0	+ 3
+ 8	8		3	+ 3
+ 8	16		6	+ 3
+ 8	24		9	+ 3
+ 8	32		12	+ 3
+ 8	40		15	+ 3
+ 8	48		18	+ 3
	56		21	

2. There are 35 students in the 7 rows of a classroom. Complete this statement.

   The classroom has ___5 students___ per ___row___.

Solve each problem.

Show your work.

3. Alex drives 10 miles in 15 minutes. How long does it take him to drive 30 miles at the same rate?

   45 minutes

4. Rosie had $35. She gave 80% of her money to her sister. How much money did Rosie have left?

   $7

5. A bag of 25 buttons contains 9 yellow buttons. If one button is picked from the bag, what is the probability that it is yellow? Express your answer as a percent.

   36%

Is each pair of figures similar? Write *yes* or *no*.

6.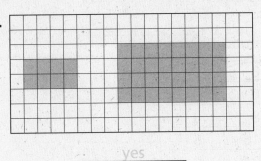

_____ yes _____

7.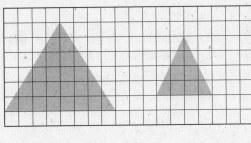

_____ no _____

8. This scale drawing shows that the distance from Woodbridge to Elmhurst is 60 km. What is the distance from Woodbridge to Oaklawn?

_____ 100 km _____

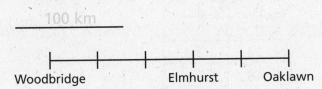

Woodbridge   Elmhurst   Oaklawn

9. Write the missing measurement.

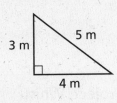

3 m   5 m   4 m

10 m   6 m   8 m

Show your work.

10. Extended Response Write a word problem for the proportion and show how to solve the problem.

$n : 39 = 7 : 21$

n = 13; Sample response: Farmer Bob's hens lay 7 brown eggs for every 21 white eggs. If he collected 39 white eggs one morning, how many brown eggs did he collect?

*Item 25 also assesses the Process Skills of Connections and Reasoning and Proof.

Math Expressions
A119
Unit 11 Test, Form A

1. A baker is making cookies. The recipe calls for 8 cups of walnuts for every 3 cups of raisins. Which is a Ratio Table for this situation?

Ⓐ

Walnuts	Raisins
3	8
0	0
3	8
6	16
9	24
12	32
15	40

Ⓑ

Walnuts	Raisins
8	3
0	0
8	3
16	6
24	9
32	12
40	15

Ⓒ

Walnuts	Raisins
8	3
0	0
8	1
16	2
24	3
32	4
40	5

Ⓓ

Walnuts	Raisins
8	3
0	0
24	3
48	6
72	9
96	12
120	15

2. Laura has 54 red stars in 6 rows glued to a board for an art project. Which sentence is true?

Ⓕ Laura has 6 red stars per row.

Ⓖ Laura has 9 red stars per row.

Ⓗ Laura has 48 red stars per row.

Ⓚ Laura has 54 red stars per row.

Solve.

3. Amanda knits 4 purple hats for every 7 green hats. She has 63 green hats. How many purple hats does she have?

   Ⓐ 32 purple hats   Ⓑ 36 purple hats   Ⓒ 56 purple hats   Ⓓ 67 purple hats

4. Jenny had $65 when she went to the carnival. She spent 80% of her money. How much did she have left after she went to the carnival?

   Ⓕ $57   Ⓖ $52   Ⓗ $25   Ⓚ $13

5. A bag of 25 marbles contains 7 clear marbles. If one marble is picked from the bag, what is the probability that it is clear? Express your answer as a percent.

   Ⓐ 21%   Ⓑ 25%   Ⓒ 28%   Ⓓ 72%

Is each pair of figures similar?

6.

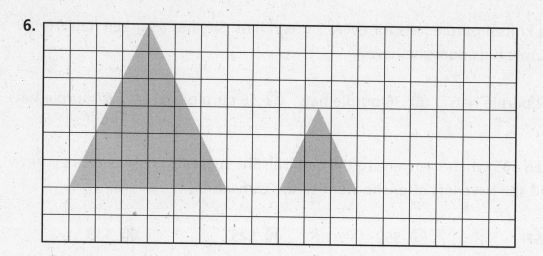

Ⓕ yes   Ⓖ no

7.

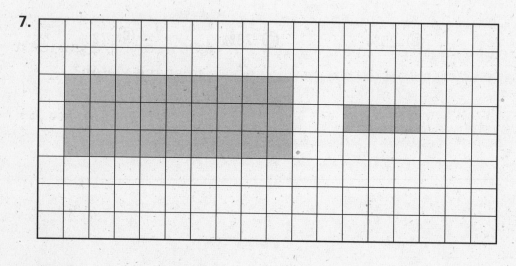

Ⓐ yes   Ⓑ no

8. This scale drawing shows that the distance from Colinwood to Mayfair is 60 km. What is the distance from Colinwood to Euclid?

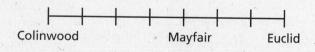

Colinwood   Mayfair   Euclid

Ⓕ 120 km   Ⓖ 105 km   Ⓗ 90 km   Ⓚ 75 km

9. What is the missing measurement?

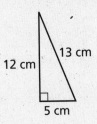

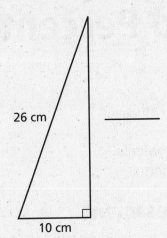

Ⓐ 36 cm   Ⓑ 26 cm   Ⓒ 24 cm   Ⓓ 18 cm

10. Nine yellow tomatoes grow for every 27 red tomatoes in Cora's garden. This season, 36 red tomatoes grew in her garden. Which proportion could you use to find out how many yellow tomatoes grew in Cora's garden this season?

Ⓕ $n : 9 = 27 : 36$ Ⓖ $n : 27 = 9 : 36$ Ⓗ $n : 27 = n : 9$ Ⓚ $n : 36 = 9 : 27$

Ratio, Proportion, and Percent

What Is Assessed
- Solve problems involving ratios.
- Apply unit rates.
- Solve proportion word problems.
- Solve problems using percents.

Explaining the Assessment

1. Tell students that they will be deciding how to share the profits of an after-school business. Profit is the total money earned minus the total expenses.

2. Read the activity aloud with the class.

Possible Responses

Question 1: The total time doing chores is 29 hours.
 The rate of pay is $5 per hour, so the total earnings are $145.
 The expenses are $10 + $15 = $25.
 The profit is $145 − $25 = $120.

Question 2: Tables may vary.
 This is one possibility.

Name	Hours	Profit
Mindra	21	
Teri	15	
Total	36	$120

Students may then use a Factor Puzzle to find Mindra's share.

		Hours	Earnings
		3	10
Mindra	7	21	(70)
Total	12	36	120

Teri's share is $120 − $70 = $50.
The shares are fair because they are in proportion to the hours worked.

Question 3: $\frac{70}{120} \approx \frac{58}{100}$. Mindra gets approximately 58%, so Teri gets approximately 42%.

Unit 11 Performance Assessment

ACTIVITY **Fair Shares**
. . . .

Mindra and Teri do neighborhood chores after school for $5 per hour. Sometimes they work together and sometimes separately.

One month, Mindra spent 5 hours knocking on doors to line up work. Teri spent 2 hours making ads to post in the neighborhood.

They charged $5 per hour for their services.

They spent $10 on paper and printing the ads and $15 on cleaning supplies.

Mindra did chores for 16 hours that month and Teri did chores for 13 hours.

1. How much profit did they make?

2. Make a table to show the hours worked and the profits. Show a fair way to share the profits. Explain your answer.

3. Estimate what percent of the total profits each person should get. Show your work.

Unit 11 Performance Assessment

Performance Assessment Rubric

An Exemplary Response (4 points)

- Uses rate, ratio, and proportion appropriately
- Includes completely accurate calculations
- Considers all contributions to the effort
- Expresses all answers in correct form with units or percent signs
- Shows a proportional basis for distributing fair shares, and explains clearly why the shares are fair

A Proficient Response (3 points)

- Uses rate, ratio, and proportion appropriately
- Includes mostly accurate calculations
- Considers all contributions to the effort
- Expresses all answers in correct form with units or percent signs
- Shows a proportional basis for distributing fair shares

An Acceptable Response (2 points)

- Uses rate, ratio, and proportion appropriately most of the time
- Includes some errors in calculations
- Considers all contributions to the effort
- Expresses almost all answers in correct form with units or percent signs
- Shows a proportional basis for distributing fair shares

A Limited Response (1 point)

- May not use rate, ratio, and proportion appropriately
- Includes many errors in calculations
- Does not consider contributions to the effort other than hours doing chores
- Does not express answers in correct form with units or percent signs
- May show an arbitrary distribution of shares

1. This is one part of a net for a rectangular prism. Complete the net.

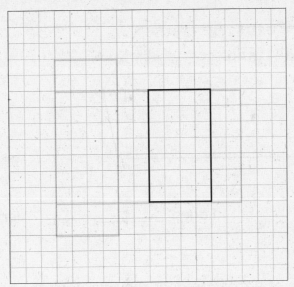

More than one answer is possible. Sample answer is shown. Check
students' drawings.

2. Toni drew this net of a cylinder. What mistake did she make?

She drew both bases on the same end of the cylinder.

3. Name the shape of the base and use it to name the pyramid.

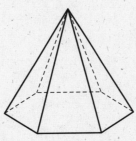

Base: _____hexagon_____   Type of Pyramid: _hexagonal pyramid_

Name: _____hexagonal pyramid_____

4. Count the faces, edges, and vertices of this figure.

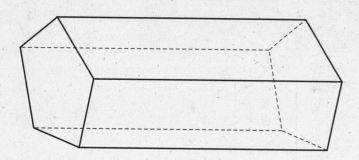

Faces: ___7___   Edges: ___15___   Vertices: ___10___

5. After what fraction of a rotation does the solid look the same? _1/4 of a rotation_

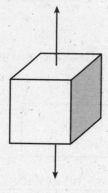

● Name each solid.

1.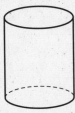

cylinder
_____

2.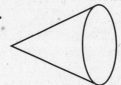

cone
_____

Name the shape of the base. Then name the solid.

3.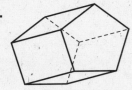

pentagon; pentagonal prism
_____

4.

rectangle; rectangular pyramid
_____

● 5.

rectangle; rectangular prism
_____

6.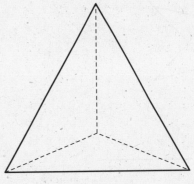

triangle; triangular pyramid
_____

Find the surface area of each three-dimensional figure.

7.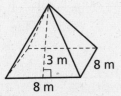

3 m   8 m

8 m

Show your work.

● surface area = ____ 112 sq m ____

8.

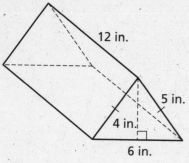

12 in.

5 in.

4 in.

6 in.

surface area = _____ 216 sq in.

Solve.

9. A cube has a surface area of 486 square inches.

What is the area of one face? _____ 81 square inches

What is the length of one edge? _____ 9 inches

Name the solid each net makes.

10.

_____ hexagonal pyramid

11.

_____ cone

12.

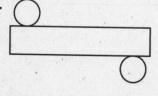

_____ cylinder

13.

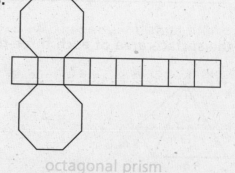

_____ octagonal prism

Math Expressions

A130

Unit 12 Test, Form A

14. Draw the top view of the stack of cubes.

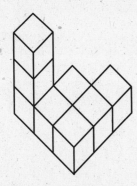   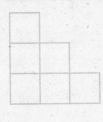

Complete the table to show the number of faces, edges, and vertices of each solid.

		Solid	Base's Sides	Faces	Edges	Vertices
15.		triangular prism	3	5	9	6
16.		square pyramid	4	5	8	5
17.		pentagonal prism	5	7	15	10

18. Will this solid look the same after $\frac{1}{2}$ of a rotation? ___yes___

Will it look the same after $\frac{1}{4}$ of a rotation? ___no___

Will it look the same after $\frac{3}{4}$ of a rotation? ___no___

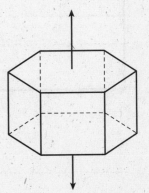

19. Draw a net of a triangular pyramid.

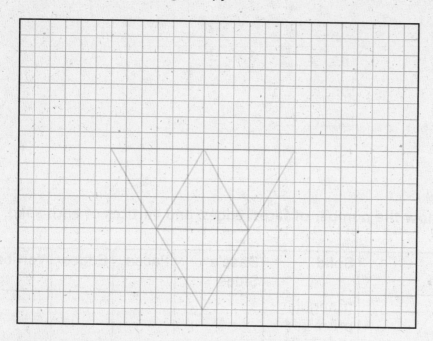

20. Extended Response Name the figure.

_____hexagonal prism_____

Draw the views of the figure.

Front	Side	Top

Math Expressions   **A132**

Unit 12 Test, Form A

Fill in the circle for the correct answer.

What is the name of each solid?

1.

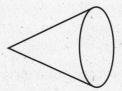

Ⓐ cone   Ⓑ cylinder   Ⓒ pentagonal prism   Ⓓ rectangular pyramid

2.

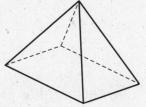

Ⓕ cone   Ⓖ cylinder   Ⓗ pentagonal prism   Ⓚ rectangular pyramid

3.

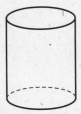

Ⓐ cone   Ⓑ cylinder   Ⓒ pentagonal prism   Ⓓ rectangular pyramid

4.

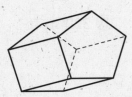

Ⓕ cone   Ⓖ cylinder   Ⓗ pentagonal prism   Ⓚ rectangular pyramid

5.

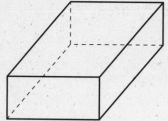

(A) cylinder   (B) rectangle   (C) square prism   (D) rectangular prism

6.

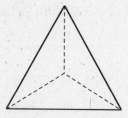

(F) triangular prism   (G) triangular pyramid   (H) cone   (K) rectangular prism

What is the surface area of each three-dimensional figure?

7.

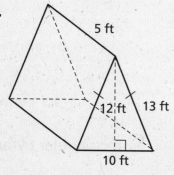

5 ft   12 ft   13 ft   10 ft

(A) 120 sq ft   (B) 180 sq ft   (C) 250 sq ft   (D) 300 sq ft

8.

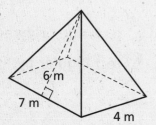

6 m   7 m   4 m

(F) 21 sq m   (G) 76 sq m   (H) 94 sq m   (K) 112 sq m

Math Expressions
A134
Unit 12 Test, Form B

9. A cube has a surface area of 384 square inches. What is the area of one face?

Ⓐ 8 square inches Ⓑ 64 square inches Ⓒ 36 square inches Ⓓ 48 square inches

Which solid does each net make?

10.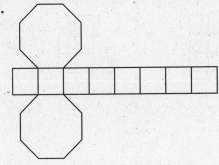

Ⓕ pentagonal prism Ⓖ rectangular pyramid

Ⓗ octagonal prism Ⓚ hexagonal pyramid

Which solid does each net make?

11.

Ⓐ cone Ⓑ cylinder Ⓒ pentagonal prism Ⓓ rectangular pyramid

12.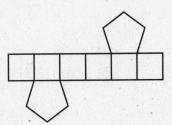

Ⓕ cone Ⓖ cylinder Ⓗ pentagonal prism Ⓚ rectangular pyramid

13.

Ⓕ cone Ⓖ cylinder Ⓗ square prism Ⓚ square pyramid

14. Which figure shows the top view of the stack of cubes?

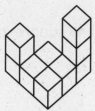

 (F)   (G)   (H)   (K)

15. How many edges does this solid have?

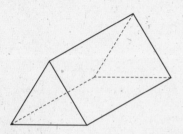

(A) 5   (B) 7   (C) 8   (D) 9

16. How many faces does this solid have?

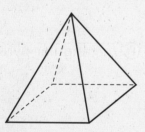

(F) 5   (G) 6   (H) 7   (K) 8

17. How many vertices does this solid have?

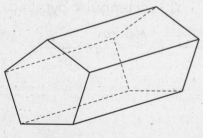

(A) 7   (B) 9   (C) 10   (D) 12

18. How many faces does an octagonal pyramid have?

    (F) 10   (G) 9   (H) 8   (K) 6

19. Does this solid have rotational symmetry?

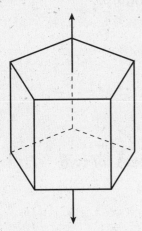

    (A) No, the solid does not have rotational symmetry.

    (B) Yes, the solid looks the same after $\frac{1}{2}$ of a rotation.

    (C) Yes, the solid looks the same after $\frac{1}{4}$ of a rotation.

    (D) Yes, the solid looks the same before a full 360° rotation.

20. Which figure shows the top view of this rectangular pyramid?

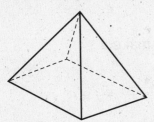

  (F) 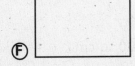 (G)  (H) 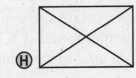 (K)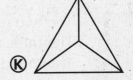

Three-Dimensional Figures

What Is Assessed

- Compare and contrast three-dimensional figures.
- Recognize, use, and create nets for three-dimensional figures.
- Find the surface area of prisms.

Materials

Centimeter ruler, paper or board at least 25 cm × 20 cm

Explaining the Assessment

1. Tell students that they will be comparing the surface areas for two prisms.

2. Read the task aloud with the class.

3. For question 2, have them draw an equilateral triangle with sides 8 cm and measure its height to the nearest centimeter.

Possible Responses

Question 1: Both are 24 cm.

Question 2: The height of the triangle is measured at about 7 cm, so its area is $\frac{1}{2} \times 7 \times 8 = 28$ sq cm.

Question 3: Check that students' nets will really fold to make a cube without duplicating any faces.

Question 4: Check that students' nets will really fold to make a triangular prism without overlapping any faces.

Question 5: The cube has the greater surface area.

The cube has a surface area of $6 \times 6 \times 6 = 216$ sq cm.

The two triangles total 56 sq cm.
The three rectangles total $3 \times 6 \times 8 = 144$ sq cm.
The total surface area of the triangular prism is about 200 sq cm.

ACTIVITY Compare Surface Areas

· ·

This square and this equilateral triangle have the same perimeter.

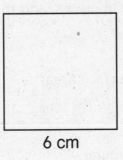 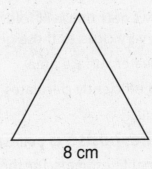

6 cm   8 cm

1. What is the perimeter of each figure?

   _____   _____

2. On paper, draw a triangle with all three sides 8 cm long. Measure its height and find its area.

   _____

   _____

3. Draw a net for a cube with sides 6 cm long.

4. Draw a net for a triangular prism. Make the sides of the triangles 8 cm long. Make the prism 6 cm long, the same length as the cube. Mark sides to show they are the same length.

5. Predict which figure will have the greater surface area. Check your prediction by calculating.

   _____

   _____

   _____

   _____

     Unit 12 Performance Assessment

Performance Assessment Rubric

An Exemplary Response (4 points)

- Makes a close estimate for the triangular area
- Accurately draws nets that will fold to build prisms, and that have measurements very close to those given
- Predicts the greater surface area
- Accurately and efficiently calculates the surface areas

A Proficient Response (3 points)

- Makes a reasonable estimate for the triangular area (within 10 sq cm)
- Draws nets that will fold to build prisms
- May not predict the greater surface area
- Accurately calculates the surface areas

An Acceptable Response (2 points)

- Makes a poor estimate for the triangular area (not within 10 sq cm)
- Draws one net that will fold to build a prism
- May not predict the greater surface area
- Accurately calculates the surface area of the cube

A Limited Response (1 point)

- Makes a poor estimate for the triangular area (not within 20 sq cm)
- Does not draw nets that will fold to build prisms
- May not predict the greater surface area
- Does not accurately calculate the surface areas